Reynard the Fox

Twayne's World Authors Series

Egbert Krispyn, Editor, The Netherlands
University of Georgia

TWAS 673

Reynard the Fox

By Thomas W. Best

University of Virginia

Twayne Publishers • Boston

Reynard the Fox

Thomas W. Best

Copyright © 1983 by G.K. Hall & Company
All Rights Reserved
Published by Twayne Publishers
A Division of G. K. Hall & Company
70 Lincoln Street
Boston, Massachusetts 02111

Book Production by John Amburg
Book Design by Barbara Anderson

Printed on permanent/durable acid-free
paper and bound in The United States
of America.

Library of Congress Cataloging in Publication Data

Best, Thomas W.
    Reynard the Fox.

    (Twayne's world authors series: TWAS 673)
    Bibliography: p. 171
    Includes index.
    1. Reynard the Fox.   I. Title.   II. Series.
PN690.R5B4   1983   809'.9336   82–13095
ISBN 0–8057–6520–4

Contents

About the Author

Thomas W. Best is an associate professor of German at the University of Virginia. He has published on medieval, Renaissance, and Baroque literature in Germany, the Netherlands, and France. Other volumes by him in the Twayne World Authors Series are on the sixteenth-century dramatist Macropedius and on the seventeenth-century dramatist Jacob Bidermann.

Preface

Medieval animal epics dealing with Reynard the Fox comprise an international body of literature which dates from approximately 1150 to 1500. These works are therefore of historical importance, but many of them also have great literary value. I have written the present book as an introduction to the major Reynard poems, which form a definite progression. The Latin *Ysengrimus* influenced many parts of the French *Roman de Renart* [Romance of Reynard], out of which the Dutch *Van den Vos Reynaerde* [Of Reynard the Fox] developed. With further help from the *Roman de Renart*, *Van den Vos Reynaerde* was expanded into the Dutch *Reinaerts Historie* [Reynard's History], which was reworked in Low German as *Reynke de Vos* [Reynard the Fox].

My book presumes no prior knowledge of medieval beast epics, being descriptive as well as analytical, but it also offers new interpretations. Rather than a summary of previous research, it is a statement of my own opinions, as grounded in previous research.

Because of restrictions on space, notes are held to a minimum and my bibliography lists only the most basic editions and studies. Although my spelling of the animals' names remains consistent with regard to any given work, it does vary from language to language and in some cases even from *Van den Vos Reynaerde* to *Reinaerts Historie*. Thus "Tibeert" is not "Tibert" misspelled, for instance, but designates the cat in one of the Dutch poems rather than in the *Roman de Renart*.

Had Egbert Krispyn not proposed this fox hunt, years ago, it would never have been ventured. My thanks to him for a grand, though arduous, experience. To Jenny de Vries, for providing me with material, and to Donald Yates, for generous help despite our differing views of *Ysengrimus,* I am also deeply grateful.

Thomas W. Best

University of Virginia

Chronology

Chapter One
Ysengrimus

The first of the Reynard epics was probably completed in 1148 or 1149 by a man at Ghent whom a later collection of aphorisms identifies as one Master Nivardus.[1] *Ysengrimus* is not the oldest medieval animal story, for fables were being created as early as the Merovingian Age and longer narratives about animals date from Carolingian times. During the second quarter of the eleventh century, we may assume, the *Ecbasis Cuiusdam Captivi* [Flight of a Certain Captive] was written, relating in well over a thousand hexameters a parable about a calf that escaped from its stall and was kidnapped by a wolf but rescued by an army of other beasts. *Ysengrimus*, in 3,287 elegiac couplets, differs conspicuously from preceding animal tales, however, not only because of its length but also because of its names. In it, for example, the fox is no longer anonymous; instead, he is christened Reinardus, for which reason we can speak of Nivardus's poem as the first Reynard epic. Ysengrimus is the wolf. In fact, nearly every beast of any prominence in the work is distinguished with a proper name. While some names were replaced in subsequent Reynard epics, others remained at least essentially the same. The fox and the wolf, respectively, continued to be called by some variant of Reinardus and Ysengrimus.

The sources of Nivardus's names is a matter of pure conjecture. He probably coined most of them himself, but he must have taken a few from folklore. That a wolf was sometimes referred to as Isengrin by the year 1112 in France is clearly documented,[2] and a woman in one scene from *Ysengrimus* terms ganders Gerarduses and hens Tetas, as if such poultry were commonly so denominated.[3] Whereas Reynard became the most popular beast in medieval French, Dutch, and German literature after 1175

and so popular in France that *renard* supplanted *goupil* as the
standard word for "fox," the wolf seems to have been more familiar
until 1150. Nivardus does not at once identify him, in contrast
to Reinardus and the other animals we meet.

Ysengrimus comprises a series of episodes, each of which is a
self-contained anecdote. In most of them the wolf suffers because
of his greed and stupidity, which are usually encouraged by
Reinardus's misleading advice. Ysengrimus enjoys his sole success
in the first little story, and in the final one he dies. The origins
of Nivardus's episodes are as uncertain as the provenance of his
names. With some we are aware of possible or partial sources;
with others we are altogether ignorant of antecedents; but in
every case we can assume that the author combined imagination
with written material or folklore, neither inventing entirely nor
timidly copying.

In order to study his extensive epic, we must break it up. Of
the five extant manuscripts—designated A, B, C, D, and E—
A separates *Ysengrimus* into seven books, while C, D, and E split
it into four. Manuscript B has no divisions at all.[4] Since A is the
oldest and best text, its format is likely to be authentic, even
though its Books I and IV each conclude in the middle of an
episode.[5] Whereas Franz Joseph Mone kept the arrangement of
Manuscripts C, D, and E in his *editio princeps* of 1832,[6] Ernst
Voigt reverted to the seven books of Manuscript A in his critical
edition of 1884 (note 1 to this chapter). We will follow Voigt
as far as content is concerned but divide the poem into its con-
stituent tales. Just how many of them there are has been a further
controversial point, with most scholars opting for twelve, as
initially proposed by Jacob Grimm.[7] We will find, however, that
fourteen are actually included.

The Ham (Book I, Verses 1–528)

Instead of presenting his episodes chronologically, Nivardus
began with the fifth one in order of time, reserving the earliest
four (pilgrimage, Sprotinus, monastery, and wolf den) for later
narration. Such inversion is a common feature of epics, including
Ecbasis Captivi, and was recommended by medieval critics. Our

author is nevertheless unorthodox in not introducing his material at all. With no preliminaries he sets us in medias res.

Early one morning, we are told (and it seems to be late in autumn),[8] Ysengrimus surprises the fox while the two of them are searching for food. To save himself, Reinardus offers his "uncle," as he likes to call the wolf, three-quarters of a ham which he sees a peasant carrying. By acting lame he induces the man to chase him and discard the meat, which Ysengrimus spirits away. When the fox returns for his share, however, all that remains is the withe by which the ham was hung. Since the wolf argues that he has merely behaved like the good monk he was earlier in the year (i.e., in the monastery episode), the first anecdote establishes him as a greedy religious—Nivardus's chief target in the epic as a whole. Seeming to speak for his author, Reinardus bitterly pardons Ysengrimus by observing that it is customary for stronger and richer creatures to win out over weaker and poorer ones.

No older narrative is known about a fox being cheated of a ham he has acquired by misleading its owner, though accounts of a bird obtaining food for an animal by feigning injury have been widespread. Two other kindred matters that were also popular will occupy us later. One concerns a fox who tricks fish merchants by playing dead, as in *Branche* III of the *Roman de Renart,* and the second is the lion's-share theme, which Nivardus used for his twelfth episode. Voigt calls attention, moreover, to a fable in Egbert of Liège's moralizing Latin reader from circa 1023, *Fecunda Ratis.*[9] There a wolf refuses to share hams—found in some unexplained fashion—with a fox and a lark.

Ice Fishing (Book I, Verses 529–1064 and Book II, Verses 1–158)

The first adventure leaves Reinardus hungrier for vengeance than for food when he meets the wolf one Saturday evening in coldest February. They show that they have had no contact in the intervening months by joking about the ham. If the fox is bringing something else, says Ysengrimus, he will split it fairly this time, but Reinardus replies, in part, that the wolf should not share anything, being insatiable, and ought to dine more on fish, having previously been a monk. Ysengrimus agrees.

At dusk they reach a frozen pond, and Reinardus instructs the wolf to stick his tail, which will serve as a net, through a crack in the ice. Surprisingly, dawn is already breaking when Ysengrimus settles down to business, so the fox departs for a neighboring village, where Mass is about to be celebrated by a shabby priest named Bovo. Reinardus snatches Bovo's rooster and dashes toward the pond, causing the curé to shout that his parishioners must join in pursuit if they want his prayers. "A thousand" do, according to Nivardus, and Reinardus is bombarded with everything that can be taken from the church, including crosses and the missal, which Bovo himself contributes.

Thus the fox must not be far ahead of the worshipers, whom he does not yet want to outrun, but when he reaches the pond he is able to converse with Ysengrimus for no less than 159 lines before the mob bursts in upon them. Nivardus simply freezes Bovo and company for five minutes of suspended animation while Reinardus gleefully exhorts the wolf to flee and Ysengrimus realizes that he cannot. When the fox has sported enough, Nivardus releases the horde, to interrupt Reinardus's final word as if realism were scrupulously respected. The time having come to elude his pursuers, the chicken thief vanishes with his prize. While dining in a hillside burrow above the pond, he watches the wolf being teased and thrashed.

Book II begins with Ysengrimus's tormentors dropping from fatigue, except for a fury named Aldrada. Foaming with rage, she swings an ax at the wolf, but he flings himself onto his back, so that she misses. Before a second try she invokes a string of saints, many of whom are fanciful and with all of whom she associates superstition or misinformation, to heighten Nivardus's satire on peasant ignorance. [10] After also mispronouncing seven phrases from the Mass, she hefts her ax again, only to let it slip, cutting the wolf loose instead of splitting his body. The author crowns his contemptuous portrayal of her by having her fall in such a way that her lips touch the stump of Ysengrimus's tail and her nose, his anus. Taking neither leave nor fish, says Nivardus, the wolf bounds away.

This episode is the first recorded version of a far-reaching folk tale, in which Ysengrimus seems to have replaced a bear. The anecdote probably originated as an explanation for why bears have short tails.[11] The motif of fishing with a tail as a net, however, dates from as early as approximately A.D. 200, when Claudius Aelianus imputed it to foxes in his Greek encyclopedia of nature lore, *On the Characteristics of Animals* (6:24).

The Surveyor (Book II, Verses 159–688)

The action continues with no time lapse, as the wounded wolf unknowingly wanders close to the den in which Reinardus is lurking. Although Ysengrimus howls for revenge, the fox emerges, to exploit his foe's voraciousness. "An empty stomach is the worst of all adversities," he philosophizes, urging the wolf to end that pain. Joseph the ram, he asserts, and the latter's three brothers want their pasture divided into four equal parts. By marking the center for them, Ysengrimus would gain an opportunity to devour them. The wolf hesitates when he sees their horns, but their lack of teeth reassures him. Swaggering into the meadow, he displays his own fangs and demands the rams for dinner. Each of them charges from a different direction and all four collide against him, nearly killing him, though fate has appointed Salaura the sow to be his executioner, Nivardus remarks in anticipation of the final episode. On Reinardus's advice the quartet add "cups" to the "dishes" served, and Book II concludes with the surveyor being battered even worse than the fisher at the end of Book I.

Whereas the ham and pond affairs have known antecedents of some kind, this third escapade does not. Avianus's eighteenth fable, which Voigt considered related,[12] merely tells of four bullocks who fall victim to a lion because they fail to stick together. The motif of dissident rams smashing an ostensibly mediating wolf has not been well liked, furthermore, and we will not encounter it again.

The Sick Lion (Book III)

In contrast to preceding episodes, Nivardus's account of how
the king of the beasts was cured rests more on a literary tradition
than on folklore, if indeed on folklore at all. According to a
Greek fable, which is probably the earliest extant version of the
incident, an aging lion lay sick in his royal cave. Every subject
came solicitously, except the fox, whom the wolf denounced as
disloyal. Having arrived in time to hear his enemy's final words,
the delinquent defended himself by claiming to have found a
remedy. The lion needed to be wrapped in the hide of a freshly
skinned wolf. When the wolf lay dead, the fox observed with a
chuckle that it is dangerous to rile a ruler. [13]

This fable seems to have been transmitted to Western Europe
by the tenth century and expanded into a poem (*Aegrum Fama
Fuit*) of thirty-four Latin distichs. Age is no longer cited there
as a factor in the lion's malaise, nor is the sufferer located any-
where, as in a cave. His vassals, many of whom are listed in lines
7–16, come "calling for doctors" but not bringing any. The fox
is not just late in arriving but disdains to appear at all, until he
has been censured by the bear, rather than by the wolf, and the
king has condemned him to death. When he is somehow apprised
of what has happened at court, he enters with a number of old
shoes strung over his shoulder, moving the lion to smile. He
explains that he wore out the shoes looking for a cure, which he
finally found but hesitates to reveal. Although the king seems
a bit skeptical, demanding disclosure only if the "sweet fox" is
telling the truth, he still lets the bear be flayed. That victim of
his own malice is not killed by his sacrifice, and instead of
commenting on how royalty should be handled, the fox concludes
by adding insult to injury. Since the bear's paws and the top of
his head have not been stripped like the rest of his body, the fox
calls him "Father" and asks who gave him his "gloves" and his
"bishop's cap." In a two-line postscript the unknown author,
terming himself "your humble servant," offers his art to an unnamed benefactor with the admonition to consider diligently
what it means. [14]

More rewarding for us is to ponder, instead, why the author introduced his innovations. The lion is not said to be old or to lie in a cave because the poem was written for some important personage who was supposed to identify with the animals' lord but not to take umbrage. The catalog of faithful subjects impresses us with their numbers, in contrast to the lone nonconformist. He is more remiss in order that he may be thought to have hiked farther, consulting more physicians, and his death sentence both forces him to court and makes more dramatic the reversal which results. The wolf is replaced by the bear because a bear's hide will better cover a lion, unless the poem was composed as a satire on some specific courtier who resembled a bear more than a wolf. The lion's proviso, "if you are telling the truth, sweet fox," was inserted to suggest that the monarch (and consequently the author's patron) is not gullible, despite accepting the fox's advice. Implied is the idea that His Majesty is giving a favorite the benefit of doubt both in desperation and because an envious rival deserves to be punished. Death, after all, is not a consequence here. The fox's raillery at the end is more in character than his Greek counterpart's moralization.

At the beginning of this chapter *Ecbasis Captivi* was mentioned. One of the beasts besieging the wolf there at least on the pretext of liberating the captive calf is the fox, whom the wolf particularly fears. His cave once belonged to an ancestor of the fox, who now hopes to regain it. To his attendants, the otter and the hedgehog, the wolf relates how the fox's forbear initially acquired the cave. That story, comprising most of the epic (lines 392–1097),[15] is another elaboration of the sick-lion fable but one which contains a great deal of extraneous material. The following paragraph summarizes elements of it important for Nivardus's heritage.

Struck with a kidney ailment, the lion ordered all his subjects to attend him in his cave. The wolf, as chamberlain, took a census of everyone present and reported the fox's absence to the king, adding a false charge of treason, even though the fox was his nephew. Accordingly the absentee was condemned to death, whereupon the wolf prepared a gallows for him. Disturbed by this turn of events, the panther alerted the fox, who came and

told the lion that he had been in Palestine, where a coot informed
him of the malady. Despite advancing age, the fox asserted (and
also despite the amount of time involved), he searched the earth
in the king's behalf, eventually finding a remedy. The lion was
to be warmed by his chamberlain's hide after the fox had smeared
his back with a fish brain allegedly brought from India. The
skinning was conducted by the bear and two lynxes. As in *Aegrum
Fama Fuit* some fur was left on the victim's paws and head, but
he died as in the original fable, scoffed at by the whole court
rather than by the fox alone. After being appointed regent, the
fox was granted the cave which the wolf's descendant possesses
in the framework plot but loses to the fox's offspring when the
abducted calf is liberated.

Two significant advances in this account of the lion's cure are
the panther's warning of danger instead of the fox's dependence
on fortuitous rumor, and the official summoning of subjects,
which causes the fox to disregard an actual law. Even if the
treason charge is meant to help justify the death sentence, however, that decree is issued improperly, as the fox points out in
lines 523–32, and the wolf's inflated enmity toward him is
unexplained. The *Ecbasis* author seems not to have known *Aegrum
Fama Fuit*, since the fox brings no old shoes and it is not the
wolf's "gloves" and "cap" which occasion mockery. Like the fox's
death sentence, the hide remaining on the wolf's paws and head
must derive from a source common to both poems.

Well after the creation of *Ysengrimus*, Marie de France translated
her fable book *Esope* from English into French, including a fifty-
six-line rendition of the sick-lion tale, with a four-line moral
appended (number sixty-eight in the collection). Although lost,
her source is assumed to have antedated *Ysengrimus*. [16] If so, it was
probably based on a Latin treatment of the sick-lion affair which
Nivardus could also have used. As we will see, that putative Latin
precursor is likely to have contained several new motifs shared
by *Ysengrimus*, at least in part. Regardless of the uncertainties
behind Marie's sixty-eighth fable, it deserves our attention.

In it the sick lion's subjects are summoned by the wolf as court
provost, but to a hall rather than a cave. Some of them send for

the fox in the belief that he can provide a remedy. He comes, though with no shoes and hiding first within earshot of the hall. After hearing the provost, who is not his relative, denounce him to the angry lion and demand his death as an example, he steps forth and alleges that he has been to the famous medical school at Salerno, where physicians prescribed a fresh wolf's hide as a poultice. The provost does not die from the loss of his skin, perhaps to his regret, since flies harass him and the fox makes fun of him by observing that his "gloves" are torn.

Of the elements here which are not standard, as judged by the other arrangements we have examined, the wolf's position is reminiscent of *Ecbasis Captivi;* his being overheard by the fox resembles the Greek fable; and his survival, plus the fox's mockery of him, remind us of *Aegrum Fama Fuit.* New details are the hall, the fox being privately fetched at the behest of a clique before he is accused, his supposed trip to Salerno, and flies attacking the defenceless wolf.

Although we are to ascertain that the sick-lion episode in *Ysengrimus* shares distinctive traits with *Aegrum Fama Fuit, Ecbasis Captivi*, and the original of Marie's sixty-eighth fable, we will not be able to conclude that any one of those works was definitely or primarily Nivardus's source. In all likelihood he was inspired by several antecedents, whatever they were, to create a story very much his own, and we will notice a wealth of unconventional material in his version. Since it is decidedly the longest episode in *Ysengrimus*, at 1,198 lines, and is also a book unto itself, like the final incident, Nivardus seems to have been especially fond of it.

That may be why he began it with a thirty-line introduction, though Van Mierlo has pointed out that those verses provide some transition from the previous episode.[17] After generalizing pessimistically for twenty lines on the maliciousness of fate, which tortures all of us slowly, Nivardus focuses on Ysengrimus, for whom he feigns sympathy, ironically blaming the wolf's woes on destiny rather than on greed and stupidity. At the same time he comments obliquely on the overall scheme of his epic. Fortune, he declares, will offset two kisses for Ysengrimus with ten slaps in the face, now tearing the wolf's fur, now stripping it off, but destroying him only later. The "kisses" are the two episodes (ham and Sprotinus) in which Reinardus is frustrated, while the "slaps in the face" are the ten incidents (ice-fishing, surveyor, sick-lion, pilgrimage, monastery, wolf-den, kick, swallowing-Joseph, lion's-share, and perjury) in which Ysengrimus is hurt, directly or indirectly, before being killed.[18] In the ice-fishing, surveyor, pilgrimage, monastery, kick, swallowing-Joseph, and perjury episodes the wolf's hide is damaged one way or another, besides being removed in the sick-lion and lion's-share incidents.

Though all the scenes in *Ysengrimus* are set near Ghent, where no lions roamed, a lion is still king, in keeping with tradition. Nivardus acknowledges the unnaturalness of that situation by stating that his ruler, named Rufanus, is the son of a Hungarian father and a Suevan (i.e., Balkan) mother. In the next chapter we will see that Pierre de Saint-Cloud, who was greatly influenced by Nivardus, established the lion as king in vernacular Reynard epics, so that the native bear, who has a legitimate claim to the throne by virtue of his size, never mounts it.[19] The closest he comes is in a tale concocted by Willem's fox in *Van den Vos Reynaerde* (Chapter Three), and even there he is not successful.

Rufanus becomes deathly ill of a fever in the July following that February when the fishing and surveyor episodes took place. Reclining in the shade of a deep valley, he summons his highest ranking vassals, and a large number of lesser subjects come voluntarily. To insure the safety of all travelers, a universal peace is imposed. No fighting is allowed till everyone is home again, but Reinardus will continue his indirect feud, in which some third party operates for him. On this occasion, as also in the lion's-share episode, his agent will be no less than the king, although he ignores the royal summons. As an excuse for doing so, he uses the image of himself which he introduced at the end of the ham endeavor, muttering that he is too poor and insignificant to be above contempt at court.

With fur that is still not entirely full, Ysengrimus obeys the call, presumptuously appropriating the place of honor beside the groaning lion, despite being no official at all, and loudly boasting

a knowledge of medicine. He shouts that Reinardus's pride must
be humbled for snubbing the king, whose health would be restored by the prompt consumption of Joseph and of Berfridus the
goat. Berfridus retorts that neither is suitable and that the wolf
is no better as a doctor than he was as a surveyor. Reinardus's
prescription is what is needed. Bruno the bear then intercedes
for the truant and sends Gutero the hare to fetch him. The faction
which solicits the fox in Marie's fable before the king condemns
him therefore has an equivalent here.

When he has been informed of the wolf's reproach, Reinardus
vows to turn the tables. He instructs the timorous, compliant
hare to report that he was not at home, and he gathers a number
of efficacious herbs. Taking those and some worn-out shoes, like
the fox in *Aegrum Fama Fuit*, he departs for Rufanus's valley,
although he has grown so fat in his burrow that he can hardly
walk. He seems to roll like a ball, with a figure that belies his
self-styled poverty. (He poses as a pauper simply because he is
small.)

At court he pretends to collapse with exhaustion before complaining of being unappreciated for not being rich. With a smile
that may derive from *Aegrum Fama Fuit*, Rufanus asks about his
services. Having read of the king's illness in the stars, says Reinardus, he ran to Salerno (perhaps suggested by the original
version of Marie's sixty-eighth fable), where he learned the proper
remedy and was given his herbs. He distributes these among
various vessels and purports to be bloated because he is dying
from hunger, with just enough life left to prepare Rufanus's
potion.

By alleging that he needs something else, which its miserly
owner will refuse to contribute, Reinardus teases the king into
a sufficient pique to insist that anything necessary will be obtained. For the sake of toying with his victim, the fox then states
only that Rufanus must be covered by the hide of some three-
and-a-half-year-old wolf. Ysengrimus tries twice to sneak away,
but Reinardus calls him back each time, announcing on the
second occasion that a suitable wolf is present. "What wolf is
here besides me?" Ysengrimus queries, to Joseph's and Bruno's

delight. After congratulating his "uncle" on this opportunity for distinction, the fox proclaims that Ysengrimus has just the proper age. When the latter protests that he is over 160 years old, Reinardus maintains that twelve months ago this very day, during a pilgrimage (the episode to be recounted next), he swore that he was two and a half. In an action reminiscent of *Ecbasis Captivi*, the lion orders Bruno to assist the donor in slipping out of his robe, and much like his analogues in *Aegrum Fama Fuit* and *Ecbasis Captivi*, Ysengrimus is bared everywhere except his forepaws, his nose, and the top of his head, moving several colleagues to ridicule him.

When the wolf has left the court, Rufanus drinks the medicine which has been prepared and perspires under the shaggy pelt. While recuperating, he asks the fox to entertain him with an account of the pilgrimage, Ysengrimus's stay in the monastery, and Sprotinus the rooster's trickery. Being tired, Reinardus passes the request along to Bruno, who has written a poem about his escapades. After Gutero has fetched the manuscript, Grimmo the boar reads from it. In this way Nivardus presents the next four episodes, which occurred one year earlier.

The Pilgrimage (Book IV, Verses 1–810)

Bertiliana the chamois[20] set out alone to visit holy relics. When she was halfway to Cologne on a Thursday in July, she met Reinardus, who reproached her for thinking that traveling singly is more pious. Yielding to his pressure, she was joined not only by him but also by Rearidus the stag, Berfridus, Joseph, Carcophas the ass, Gerardus the gander, and Sprotinus the cock, who were all Reinardus's companions. Not until the next episode do we learn that the goat, the ram, the gander, and the rooster had run away from home to avoid being fed to guests at a wedding, while Carcophas, who lives on the same farm with them, had fled the chore of hauling wood for that celebration, although he was laden with provisions on the trip. We are never told why Rearidus was one of the troop, nor is the fox's reason for wanting to unite with Bertiliana ever indicated. In the Sprotinus incident

we will see that he has designs on Gerardus and the cock, but
we are left to guess why he was drawn to the chamois.[21]

Lurking nearby, 160-year-old Ysengrimus overheard Reinardus
and Bertiliana and caught sight of Carcophas's load. The wolf
wanted also to become a member of the group, but he had been
eating so well of late that he was even more swollen than the fox
in the sick-lion episode. Instead of just seeming to roll, he actually
had to, for which reason the pilgrims soon outdistanced him.
Finding an empty hostel at dusk, they decided to spend the night
there, and in expectation of Ysengrimus, Reinardus took down
a wolf's head from over the door, preparing a trick with Joseph.
The ram then posted Carcophas at the entrance, instructing him
to do the opposite of what he was told, should Ysengrimus
intrude. Because the ass was too hungry to stand guard and
dashed about, *scavenging* food, the menace they had feared walked
in, his physical condition having meanwhile improved.

Although plotting mayhem, he posed as a hermit en route to
Rome and the Holy Land. Immediately he sat down to eat, so
the fox told Joseph to serve him a wolf's head. They had nothing
else, Reinardus said, and it would be good enough for a poor
recluse. The ram obeyed, playing the fox's prearranged game.
Before a queasy Ysengrimus he dangled the head which had
probably been hung to ward off evil spirits. It had belonged to
an eremite of Anjou, he claimed. Ordered to fetch a bigger one,
he returned with the same head, now tonsured, and affirmed that
he and his colleagues had recently removed it from an English
abbot. Similarly large specimens could be found in the abbeys
of Sithiu and Arras, he joked. Still not satisfied, Reinardus instructed the ram to look in the other corner, which was supposedly
full of even choicer examples, and to bring the head whose jaws
were propped open. Grumbling about having to rummage among
thousands, Joseph asked whether the fox meant the one accidentally ripped off the day before by Gerardus, who did not see its
owner, a Danish bishop, lying in the grass. "Quite right," Reinardus replied, whereupon the ram offered the same head a third
time but with a stick between its teeth and all its hair removed,
together with its ears. Ysengrimus completely lost his appetite,

and he fainted when Gerardus screamed, after bragging of the ability to decapitate nine wolves, including the one in their midst.

Not only calculated to frighten Ysengrimus and to turn his stomach, the fox's practical joke is another expression of Nivardus's antipathy toward lupine ecclesiastics. Those of Anjou, Sithiu, and Arras are stigmatized specifically, while the putative English abbot and the fanciful Danish bishop imply, as Voigt observes,[22] that wolfishness was generally widespread within the Church. The open jaws suggest particular ferocity at the episcopal level.

Now the interloper really wanted to retreat, but Reinardus reassured him, overruling Berfridus's desire to let him go. They needed Ysengrimus as a counselor, said the fox, transferring his own role to the wolf, whom he termed his uncle. Surely their new companion would not want to leave relatives, Reinardus remarked, moving Ysengrimus to contend that he was only the godchild of the fox's uncle and too young to give advice, having just turned two and a half that day. (Thus it is wrong of Reinardus to aver in the sick-lion episode that the wolf professed such a tender age one year earlier. Ysengrimus did not impute it to himself, and he should say so at court.)[23]

Since the wolf steadfastly refused to trouble his friends any longer, Reinardus exhorted Joseph, Rearidus, and Berfridus to serve him their "cups," in effect anticipating the surveyor episode. As the three preceded Ysengrimus out, Joseph directed Carcophas to open the door wide, but the ass, who remembered his earlier instructions, opened it only a little and slammed it on the wolf, pinching him in a vise. After much ironic commentary on their captive and a grotesque tootle from the goat's three horns, Joseph, Rearidus, and Berfridus butted Ysengrimus's front while Sprotinus, Gerardus, and especially Reinardus bit his rear inside the house. When finally released, the wolf threatened revenge at dawn, sneering that he and a chorus would "sing" with the pilgrims.

His return with eleven clansman constitutes a short second stage in this episode. Except for clumsy Carcophas, all the sojourners in the hostel climbed onto its roof by means of a large haystack at one side. In trying to clamber up, the ass fell down, landing on two of the wolves. Reinardus yelled that the entire dozen would soon be eaten, and Gerardus hissed, flapping his wings. Ysengrimus, whom the goose had previously scared, took to his heels in another funk. Deserted by their leader, the rest of the warriors also fled, scattering in every direction.

Although the pilgrimage is chronologically Nivardus's earliest episode, it does not include an explicit explanation for the feud between fox and wolf that underlies most of the epic. It implies, however, that Ysengrimus is the enemy of every animal, except for others of his kind and possibly the lion, on account of his rapaciousness. The author presupposed hostility between the belligerent wolf and the intelligent fox because it seemed natural in addition to being traditional, as documented by versions of the sick-lion fable (especially *Ecbasis Captivi*, where the wolf defames the fox and avidly awaits his death), and even by Claudius Aelianus, who stated in *On the Characteristics of Animals* (1:36) that foxes hate wolves since the latter scheme against them.

Nivardus's source for the pilgrimage appears to have been a combination of two fairy tales, as Antti Aarne has maintained.[24] The first told how a ram and a goat frightened wolves away by means of a wolf's head and routed them again by falling on them. The second story, a variant of which is the familiar Grimm account of the Bremen musicians, told how farm beasts running away from home took over a house belonging to wolves one night when the owners were out and put the latter to flight upon their return. The two tales were conjoined because of their common basic elements—peaceable creatures scaring wolves. Aarne assumed that Nivardus added the fox and the pilgrimage motif, as well as all of the names and Ysengrimus's pose as a hermit, but we cannot be sure.

Sprotinus (Book IV, Verses 811–1044, and Book V, Verses 1–316)

When the wolves had been disposed of and the sun had risen on Friday morning, the rooster urged Gerardus the gander to join him in abandoning the pilgrimage, since the wedding feast which

threatened both of them along with Berfridus, Joseph, and Carcophas was over. The fox had become more dangerous for them
than the farm, despite having sworn not to hurt them. Seeing
them whisper together, Reinardus asked them why they were
afraid. Ysengrimus and his cronies were gone, after all. To himself
Sprotinus thought, "But you haven't gone yet, Brother. You
want to be to me what the wolf is to you," and indeed the fox
assumes much of Ysengrimus's role in this episode, from which
his enemy is totally absent. Reinardus does not represent clerics,
and he is not physically abused, but he is an evil menace, and
he is out-witted. Reproaching the gander and the cock for their
mistrust, he demanded that the three of them renew their pledge
of good faith. To allay his suspicions, Sprotinus consented,
though still slipping off with Gerardus at the first opportunity.
While Bertiliana, Rearidus, Carcophas, Joseph, and Berfridus
continued their pilgrimage, the rooster and the gander headed
home but not together, since the plot requires that Sprotinus be
alone. In his indifference toward technicalities Nivardus did not
bother to advance any reason for why two fowl who live on the
same farm and fear a common peril would not keep each other
company.

Finding the rooster in a barn somewhere, Reinardus played on
both his courage and his pride (key traits in any cock) by scoffing
that he was too timid to equal his father, who could sing mag-
nificently while standing on one leg with one eye closed. Sprotinus
showed that he could do the same. His sire could also crow on
one leg with both eyes closed, however, being heard to the limits
of God's control and even thirty-two miles beyond, the fox declared. In attempting to meet that challenge, too, the cock was
seized.

Rather than spoil Nivardus's plot by downing his prize on the
spot, which seems to have been secure enough, Reinardus carried
the rooster off, enabling peasants on whatever farm they were to
catch sight of them and give chase. The men also gave Sprotinus
a means of beating the fox at his own game, for they called
Reinardus a thief. If he were of masterful stock, the cock chided,
he would tell those boors that he was taking his rightful property.

Of course, in order to be able to shout, he would have to drop his prey, but Sprotinus vowed not to dare escape, terming it useless. The fox was so complacent that he heeded the rooster. As he asserted his rights in defiance of the crowd, which immediately vanished, its function in the story fulfilled, the rooster flew to the top of a bramble bush. There he crowed triumphantly in Hungarian, Greek, and Chaldean, consoling his dupe with an offer of blackberries. Reinardus departed momentarily on the pretext of ascertaining whether peace had been instituted, at which point Book IV ends.

At the outset of Book V Nivardus comments on the fox, making three points: (1) hardly anyone is always wise; (2) Reinardus blundered in defending his honor; and (3) a wise deceiver deceived, publicly concealing his chagrin, does not give up. Though he acted nonchalant with Sprotinus, the fox raged in private, viciously biting an old shoe and cursing his teeth for not having treated the rooster in the same way. They should be as greedy as the pope, he hissed, or better, as greedy as Anselm, the bishop of Tournay (1146–49, Nivardus's own bishop!), but not like those senseless apostles Peter and Paul or that poor fool Bernard of Clairvaux. In the same ironic manner Reinardus "praised" the acquisitive rich in general as true nobility, while calling poverty the sole disgrace of the age.

A second stage in this episode begins when he discovered a piece of birch bark in the form of a royal missive and ran back to Sprotinus with it. Despite assurances of having nothing more to fear because Rufanus's barons had indeed established peace, the cock was not to be convinced, even when his adversary pretended to read from the "proclamation" that skeptics would be put to death. From the height of his bramble bush Sprotinus purported to discern a hunter on horseback approaching with dogs. Maybe they were imperial messengers bearing word of the new decree, he smirked.

Though growing uneasy, the fox still tried a third time to beguile his elusive prey. Because bells were tolling in the distance, he alleged that the festival of Saint Machutus[25] was to be held the next day, also imposing a truce, but Sprotinus insisted on waiting for what the rider would report. After enough further dialog to permit the hunter to arrive if he really did exist, Reinardus fled in disgrace.

The episode's first stage, which eventually became Chaucer's "Nun's Priest's Tale," stands in a long line of literary development, like the sick-lion incident. In a couple of Greek fables a cock outwits a fox, but his situation is not the same as Sprotinus's.[26] Much more similar is a Latin fable of uncertain though very early age. It relates that a fox, after complimenting a partridge on her beauty, added that she would be even more stunning asleep. When the vain bird closed her eyes, the fox seized her, but she regained enough presence of mind to plead that her name be spoken before she perished. The fox condescended to say "partridge," whereupon the partridge escaped, reproaching herself for having shut her eyes, while the fox was disgusted at having opened his mouth.[27]

Charlemagne's friend Alcuin, who died in 804, wrote a Latin poem in thirty-three hexameters (*Versus de Gallo*) about a rooster snatched by a wolf. Like the partridge, the cock makes a last request, but one more appropriate for an authority on voice. He wants to know whether what he has heard of the wolf's fantastic vocal ability is true. The flattered abductor howls, and his dinner flies away, to lecture him on pride.[28] Alcuin replaced the usual chicken chaser with a wolf because his story hinges on operatic talent.

In an eleventh-century poem (*Gallus et Vulpes*) of seventy-two four-line stanzas a cock crowing on a manure pile attracts a hungry fox. The prowler praises him as a match for his father except that the latter could supposedly pirouette while singing. The son demonstrates that he can, too, and the fox acts suitably impressed, though alleging that the elder rooster could also close an eye. The younger does so, as well, over which stunt the fox affects a swoon. On recovering, he declares that the cock would become supreme by crowing and pirouetting with both eyes shut. During this feat he grabs the performer and runs, with a band of peasants close behind. They are accusing him of thievery, the cock tells the fox, and the rooster acts insulted by the insinuation that a robber will consume him. He should be put down and the mob should be informed that the fox has earned him, the cock admonishes. That advice is heeded, with predictable results, and each creature curses his mistake, basically like the participants in the partridge fable. [29]

As with the sick lion, a hypothetical forerunner of the first stage in the Sprotinus episode is the lost original of a fable by Marie de France. In Chapter 60 of her *Esope* a fox lauds a rooster descanting from a dung heap but claims that the cock's father was superior because he crowed with his eyes closed. Although tricked, the son redeems himself by persuading his kidnapper to tell pursuers that he belongs to the fox. Again both of them scold themselves for their respective faults. [30]

None of these versions is quite like Nivardus's, in which there is a barn rather than a manure pile, Reinardus seduces Sprotinus in two steps rather than either one (as in the partridge fable and Marie's) or three (as in *Gallus et Vulpes*), and the cock does not chide himself. Nivardus's source, whether oral or written, must have been closest to *Gallus et Vulpes,* however, where the fox not only proceeds gradually with the rooster but also releases him intentionally before addressing peasants.

Marie de France's sixty-first fable resembles the second stage of the Sprotinus episode. A fox implores a dove perched on a cross to shelter itself from the wind by sitting with him on the ground. The dove need not be afraid of him, the fox contends, because he has just left an assembly where a letter from the king was read, terminating hostilities. "Then I'll come down," the dove teases, "but over by that grove I see two horsemen riding fast, accompanied by two dogs." The fox decides to disappear, even though he does not know whether the dove is telling the truth. To save face, he says that the hunters might not yet have learned of the royal edict. [31]

Nivardus probably did not use precisely Marie's form of this story, to judge by the discrepancies between it and his own version (in particular, Marie's fox bears no birch bark), but he was surely familiar with an equivalent tale, which is likely to have involved a dove, since that is the bird of peace, rather than

a cock. He may even have been inspired by a fable collection like
Marie's, in which the encounter between a fox and a rooster
immediately precedes the one between a dove and a fox. He
changed the dove to a cock and added the Machutus ruse, along
with lesser details. It is clear that Sprotinus is not to be tricked
a second time, but Nivardus appended the second stage in order
to impress on us Reinardus's fallibility and wickedness. Why the
fox in effect replaces the wolf on this one occasion will become
apparent later.

The Monastery (Book V, Verses 317–704)

After being frustrated by the cock, Reinardus wandered cease-
lessly for four days, still without eating, in fear of Sprotinus's
hunting dogs. At the point of collapse he met somewhere a cook
(presumably from the monastery of Saint Peter at Blandigny)
whose sheep he had once protected from Ysengrimus. In thanks
and also out of pity over his near starvation, the cook gave him
a platter full of cakes. Anticipating another encounter with the
wolf, Reinardus saved eight of them and had himself tonsured
(presumably by the cook).

Sure enough, he soon met Ysengrimus, who threatened to kill
him. Claiming to be a monk, the fox offered his cakes as a sample
of monastery cuisine, but rather than approach the dangerous
wolf, he threw the whole batch from a safe distance. Ysengrimus
swallowed them in a single gulp, platter and all, so that he hardly
knew whether he had tasted them or not, but he wanted to join
the cloister in which they were regular fare. Reinardus consequently shaved his head and took him to Blandigny, where he
made his vows and donned a cowl. His presence attracted eleven
abbots, two of whom—Walter of Egmond and Balduin of Lies-
born—Nivardus praises at length but ironically, according to
Willems and Van Mierlo.[32]

Though a priest is only figuratively a shepherd, as his brothers
reminded him, the wolf was obsessed with actual sheep. Told to
say *Dominus vobiscum,* he could only utter *cominus ovis cum* in a
mixture of Latin and Dutch translatable as "come here, sheep"
instead of "the Lord be with you." He intoned *agne* ("lamb")

rather than "amen." He assumed that singing responsories meant killing sheep. He recommended eating five raw sheep a day instead of cakes and selling all the abbey's furnishings for sheep. "I wish everything in the world were sheep!" he cried, excepting only himself.

Because Reinardus is a layman despite his pose as a religious, he is excluded from the main events of this episode, which are based on motifs collected around the central idea of the wolf as a monk.[33] Instead of presenting those events together in a single, continuous development, Nivardus spread them over two days separated by one night. Late in the first day of Ysengrimus's sojourn at Saint Peter's he interrupted it to relate an encounter between Reinardus and the wolf's family the next morning.

The Wolf Den (Book V, Verses 705–820)

Not content with causing Ysengrimus to suffer time and again, the fox took advantage of his enemy's absence from home to include the latter's wife and newborn litter in his feud. The she-wolf (the most important animal whom Nivardus did not name) had just given birth, in fact, when Reinardus entered her cave, to serve her cubs "breakfast" by urinating and defecating all over them. Before their convalescent mother could attack him he hurried away, but she called him back, saying that she wanted to kiss him good-bye. He knew that she really wanted to bite his head off, so he approached only enough to throw stones and dirt at her. In response she chased him to his own den, which is placed ironically in an idyllic setting, a *locus amoenus* modeled after the Vale of Tempe in Thessaly. So furious was she, her recent accouchement notwithstanding, that she tried to force herself through the burrow's entrance, even though it was too small for her, and she became stuck, moving Nivardus to sermonize sententiously on foolishness while the fox emerged from a second opening, to ridicule her. In a passage evidently interpolated by a very early scribe, since every surviving manuscript except A contains some version of it and even A included it initially,[34] Reinardus also raped her, pleasing her to such an extent that she joked with him as if she had never been angry and had no cause to be.

It is assumed that this episode derives from a Northern European folk tale in which the fox ravished a bear instead of a wolf,[35] despite the greater difference in size. In Marie de France's sixty-ninth fable a fox propositions a bear until she wrathfully pursues him. She becomes caught in briars, however, permitting him his way.[36] Nivardus may have changed the bear to a wolf himself, and he suppressed the rape, no doubt considering it too much in bad taste. A ribald copyist who knew his source soon added what would be an ultimate indignity to Ysengrimus's wife if her attitude were not altered to suit the Latin word *lupa,* which means both "female wolf" and "prostitute."

Even without violating her, Reinardus's behavior is reprehensible, though Nivardus seems not to have thought so. He criticizes only the she-wolf and indicates that the fox's treatment of her young is justified because they will replace their abominable sire. Reinardus is once more exclusively an agent of his author's satire rather than primarily a target of it, as with Sprotinus. In all fairness to him, we must recognize that he does no actual harm to Ysengrimus's family. In Chapter Three we will see that Reinaert the fox is accused of having blinded two of the wolf cubs with his urine, but nothing is said in Nivardus's poem about any adverse consequences of Reinardus's visit.

The Monastery, Continued
(Book V, Verses 821–1128)

At approximately the same time that the fox was calling on his family, the wolf was called upon to sing but talked of breakfast instead, causing himself to be hissed so loudly that 300 Gerarduses seemed to menace him and the abbey's lamps were extinguished. In the belief that a storm had struck, the brothers rang the chapel bells,[37] brandished sacred objects, and hid. Finally all fifty-one of them burst into laughter.

Since Ysengrimus declared that he at least wanted something to drink if he was not to eat, the tippling abbot of Saint Peter's, whom Nivardus terms a second wolf, had him taken to the wine cellar, where he opened all the casks to sample them and was later found swimming in their contents. The brothers consequently decided to expel him, but he felt that they should make him a bishop instead, on account of his outstanding covetousness. He was therefore sprinkled with fleas, draped with a horse-collar remnant as a stole, and mitered with a spittoon. In congratulation he was pounded with the stone from a mustard mill, also with a bell, and even with a horse's head, the wielder of which joked that it was a violin because the wolf's right nostril showed him to be a minstrel.[38] As Ysengrimus was voluntarily leaving Saint Peter's, the cook (presumably the same one who gave Reinardus the cakes) impaled his shoulders with a red-hot spit, calling it a bow to match the fiddle. The new bishop wandered in a daze until he happened upon his wife, still trapped in their neighbor's doorway. He pulled her loose, and they told each other what Reinardus had done to them during the past twenty-four hours.

Still reading from Bruno's poem, Grimmo says that a ham was to pacify Ysengrimus. Because the fox is ashamed for the public to know that he was victimized both by Sprotinus and the wolf, the bear stops the boar from relating further incidents, with which we are acquainted anyway. From the past we have reverted to the present, being once again in July of the story's second year.

The Stork (Book V, Verses 1129–66)

Rufanus, who is feeling lively now, orders feasting and joviality, but rather than remain at court, we look for Ysengrimus as he wends his way home. We find him coming upon the gelding Corvigarus. Before he and the horse interact, however, Nivardus describes a very brief contest that has just taken place between Corvigarus and a nameless stork. In effect, therefore, we have another episode within an episode. Whereas the wolf-den affair does not involve Ysengrimus, neither he nor Reinardus participates in this incident, which is the only one in the entire epic to exclude both of the principal characters. It is probably based on an unknown medieval fable.[39]

Corvigarus and the stork were standing in a quagmire. Nivardus states that the bird, who is not powerful, wanted to be
thought so, for which reason he splattered with his wings and
told the horse to go somewhere else, warning that he might
accidentally destroy Corvigarus's legs with his "Satanic claws"
in the muddy water. Actually, of course, the reverse was likelier
to happen, but Corvigarus yielded, bounding onto dry land.

The Kick (Book V, Verses 1167–1322)

Having had two episodes in which Reinardus functions without
Ysengrimus and one in which neither plays a part, we now have
one in which Ysengrimus acts without Reinardus. The final incident, as we will see, also dispenses with the fox, except as a
bystander. Both there and here with Corvigarus, the wolf accomplishes on his own what his counselor helps him do in his other
adventures, apart from the theft of the ham.

The horse asks him who robbed his cowl. Ysengrimus replies
that he donated it to the sick king because Corvigarus will surely
grant him a similar favor. He also wants some meat, of which
the well-fed horse has an excess. Corvigarus could run faster with
less weight, says the wolf. The gelding's rejoinder is that the
monk might be harmed by dogs, having lost his tonsure as well
as his habit, since the hair has grown back on his head. Claiming
to be secretly a barber, who hides his razors under his hooves,
Corvigarus offers a shave. When Ysengrimus objects that the
horse's shoes look more like rings stolen from the doors of Saint
Peter's, Corvigarus is willing to return them, and he extends one
foot. The wolf moves close enough to be kicked and is struck in
the middle of the forehead, where Corvigarus's shoe remains
imbedded. With a gibe at avaricious clergy both the episode and
Book V conclude.

If Nivardus's source in this instance was not a fable in the early
Latin collection known as *Romulus,* it must at least have derived
from that tale, in which a lion attempts to deceive a horse by
posing as a physician instead of attacking in his usual, forthright
manner. The horse counters with a ruse of his own, however,
pretending to have a stick in his hoof. When the lion draws near,

he is kicked like Ysengrimus. For having come as a physician instead of a butcher he feels himself properly punished. [40] Greek versions of essentially the same fable present a wolf playing doctor to an ass. [41]

Swallowing Joseph (Book VI, Verses 1–132)

In each of the previous episodes involving both Ysengrimus and Reinardus, except for the ham sharing, the fox has caused the wolf to be assailed by some group or other (peasants, rams, the court, pilgrims, and monks). Now he begins a new trend— inducing his "uncle" to be harmed by a single animal or thing (a ram, the lion, and a trap), as with Corvigarus. The three capers in question constitute Book VI. In line 53 of that book Nivardus also starts a new trend—forgoing indications of who says what. Whether he was impatient to complete his poem, as Voigt assumed, is a moot point. [42]

Rufanus has recovered, so court is adjourned, apparently in the evening of the same day on which Ysengrimus was flayed. Nearing home shortly before dawn, Reinardus finds the wolf snapping at flies that plague him like his counterpart in Marie de France's sixty-eighth fable (described above, in the section on the lion's illness). When the fox remarks that Joseph and the ram's twelve lambs should recompense Ysengrimus for the coverlet given the king, the incorrigible glutton accompanies his adviser to Joseph's stall. The ram awaits him, having been instructed by Reinardus before leaving court.

With the sun beginning to rise, Joseph tells the wolf to lean against the stall door and spread his maw like the preacher Bernard of Clairvaux. The ram says that he will then jump down Ysengrimus's throat, so that none of him is lost. Upon complying, the dolt is knocked unconscious again and taunted for not eating more. Eventually he crawls home, where he stays until his coat grows out again.

Though Nivardus could have created this episode from the surveyor incident, he evidently did not, since Slavic versions exist. [43] At least in Western Europe the notion of a wolf believing

that he could swallow a ram whole and with impunity has proved
still less popular than the idea of one as an arbitrator for rams,
perhaps being too preposterous even for fairy tales.

The Lion's Share (Book VI, Verses 133–348)

Shortly before the autumnal equinox (22 September) Reinardus
hears that the wolf is back to normal. The process of breaking
him down must be started again, for the fourth time if we consider
the pilgrimage and monastery episodes to constitute a single
period of decline. The second such period, seven months later,
would then consist of the fishing and surveyor adventures, with
the third, another five months later, comprising the court, kick,
and swallowing-Joseph episodes. This fourth stage, also composed
of three misfortunes, is the final one and includes Ysengrimus's
obliteration. It seems to span approximately the twenty-four
hours from early 21 September to the morning of 22 September,
being therefore comparable in time to the second and third stages,
each of which lasts about as long. By contrast, we may remember,
the pilgrimage and monastery episodes occur four days apart, and
each one covers roughly twenty-four hours.

Reinardus arranges the first step in Ysengrimus's destruction
by finding Rufanus when the lion goes hunting and inviting him
to breakfast with the wolf. Upon being informed of his eminent
guest, Ysengrimus is aghast, fearing to lose his fur again, and
indeed he does. Reinardus knows of a calf, which they lead into
the woods, where Ysengrimus slaughters it and splits it into three
equal parts. Because he offers the lion only one of the three,
irascible Rufanus rips off his hide.

Bidden to redivide the spoils, the fox arranges three piles of
differing quality. The best, he says, is for the king and the second
best is for the queen, who has just given birth. The third heap,
consisting of bones, is for the young cubs, Reinardus declares.
He takes only a foot for himself and leaves nothing for the wolf,
despite admitting, when questioned by the lion, that it is Ysengrimus who has taught him to share so generously. He terminates
the episode by lecturing the wolf on avarice, the prerogative of

royalty, but though he speaks of kings, Rufanus is forgotten. We never learn what the lion does.

Ysengrimus's lesson on that September morning derives from the same Aesopian fable to which we owe our English expression, "lion's share." In the original Greek the king of the beasts goes hunting with a fox and an ass. Charged with dividing their catch, the ass makes three equal piles, at which the lion becomes enraged and eats him. The fox then heaps virtually all the booty together, keeping only a bit for himself. When asked who his teacher was, he confesses, "The unfortunate ass!"[44] In Phaedrus's Latin variant, preserved essentially unchanged in the prose of *Romulus,*[45] a lion is assisted by a cow, a goat, and a sheep in killing a stag. After splitting their quarry into four parts, the lion claims it all, since his companions are too weak to stop him. Nivardus's source was obviously closer to the Greek version. Perhaps it still even kept the ass, which Nivardus replaced with his wolf. Ysengrimus is no smarter, after all, and a much more appropriate hunter.

Perjury (Book VI, Verses 349–550)

There is no time lapse whatsoever between the lion's-share episode and this one. Immediately after his harangue on greed, Reinardus contrives to have one of the wolf's feet amputated. He asserts that Carcophas's father, Balduinus, owed Ysengrimus's father his hide. Both beasts died before the debt was paid, the fox alleges, so that now Carcophas, as his father's heir, should give his hide to the newly stripped wolf.

In the course of much discussion, the ass, whom Reinardus has coached, denies owing anything and demands a sacred oath from the wolf as evidence. The fox accordingly leads his client to what is supposedly the grave of a saint but is actually a concealed trap. Because Ysengrimus is convinced that what he covets is his, he places his right forepaw on the "relics," to sanctify his oath, and is clamped fast. Of course his advocate taunts him, and in doing so Reinardus also ridicules saints, for having generally achieved their blessedness by being mercenary. The fox doubtlessly speaks for his author here, but Nivardus can hardly have scorned all saints, as Reinardus implies. The fox exaggerates for effect. He goes on to say that the saints want the wolf because they recognize him as a fellow robber. After wishing, on behalf of Nivardus, that they would capture everyone who lives like Ysengrimus, Reinardus departs with Carcophas, before the wolf escapes by biting off his foot.

This is one of the several episodes in regard to which we are ignorant of antecedents. Unlike the surveyor, stork, and swallowing-Joseph material, however, the motif of the perjurer swearing on a trap is one we will encounter in vernacular Reynard epics—*Branches* II-Va and XIV of the *Roman de Renart*.

Salaura (Book VII)

Apparently just one night intervenes between Books VI and VII. At dawn on what he later declares to be the equinox (line 55), Ysengrimus comes upon the wild pig Salaura. Since Nivardus states that she has been feeding on acorns, we must be dealing with the autumnal equinox. Claiming to want peace now that his life is drawing to a close, the wolf asks to kiss the sow, whom he calls his godmother, but she knows how deadly his "kisses" would be. It is too early, she replies, for Mass must be celebrated first. When he protests that he is the only priest around and that his lameness prevents him from conducting the service, she purports to be an abbess and promises to sing a Mass that will amaze him, if, by biting her ear, he assists in summoning her comrades. He readily acquiesces, causing her to screech so shrilly that the two of them are soon surrounded by sixty-six other swine, whose thunderous approach Nivardus compares to the advent of Gog and Magog in Revelation 20:7–9.

Continuing Salaura's joke about celebrating Mass, as if to suggest that Ysengrimus is an antichrist and his murder is a sacred act, the pigs slowly eat him alive. He implies more clearly that their cause is holy, for he likens himself to Mohammed, the archinfidel, who was also consumed by swine, according to medieval legend. Such a death is disgraceful for him, and he attempts to requite it by damning pigs to flatulence, inflicted on them by a weird hobgoblin called Agemund. His misogynous author has him also include swinish women in his curse, which supposedly has been realized.

Along with other jests, Salaura composes an epitaph for the wolf in which she states that he lies entombed in sixty-six "urns" on account of his many virtues and in which she also assigns a nonsensical time and place to his death.[46] In the same facetious manner the herd finishes him off, leaving less, says Nivardus, than the least part of a flea that has been cut into eight pieces.

Schwab holds the number of swine to be an allusion to 666, the number of the beast from the earth in Revelation 13:11–18,[47] and we have just seen that the pigs are associated with Gog and Magog, who are also allies of Satan. It therefore looks as if the swine are malefic, yet Nivardus cannot have meant to suggest that killing Ysengrimus is bad. On the contrary, ridding the world of him is a boon.

The number sixty-six refers more probably to something antithetical to the beast from the earth. Ysengrimus dies on the autumnal equinox, and 22 September is the festival of St. Mauritius and his Theban Legion, all of whom perished for Christianity. Their number is reputed to have been 6,666. In a hymn to them, Walafried Strabo exclaims that it is right for such holy men to be distinguished by sixes, for no other number is so perfect. (No other digit is the sum of its divisors.) Isidore of Seville maintains in his *Etymologiarum Libri* (3:4.2) that the number six, being perfectly formed, symbolizes the world's perfection.[48] In the *Saturnalia* (7:13.10) Macrobius calls that number "full, perfect, and divine." Its perfection explains why the world was created over a period of six days, according to Augustine in *De Civitate Dei* (11:30). The positive implications of eliminating Ysengrimus are therefore reinforced not only by Salaura's joke about celebrating Mass and by the wolf's identification with Mohammed, while the comparison of the swine to Gog and Magog is merely one of manner, not of essence, and their onrush is described from Ysengrimus's point of view.

Because Salaura sheds crocodile tears over the demise of her "loved one," Reinardus asks whether something has happened to the wolf, even though he has observed Ysengrimus's dismantlement from a hiding place. When he hears that his "uncle" is dead, he also feigns grief. Salaura offers to let him join Ysengrimus, but he declines.

At this point she delivers a 110-line jeremiad (verses 549–658) that is the key to understanding Nivardus's intentions with *Ysengrimus*. Salaura's theme is what she asserts to be the eternal conflict between God and this willingly sinful world. After a catalog of transgressions from the Old Testament, she states that Christ was sent as judge. Though He was slain, the number of good men increased temporarily. Now the earth is corrupt again, and God has once more condemned it but deigns to warn mankind before putting His sickle to the weeds. As recent portents of doom Salaura cites a number of natural wonders, especially a terrible storm in Friesland.

The earnestness of her homily compels us to believe that she is expressing Nivardus's sincere sentiments, which prove him to have been deeply devout, if more in the mold of an Old Testament prophet than of Christ. She refutes the theory, first proposed by Max Wehrli and then elaborated by Fritz Peter Knapp, that Nivardus was a secularized freethinker.[49] Anyone reluctant to accept a pig as the author's spokesman, particularly in religious matters, should weigh these additional considerations: in order to identify Ysengrimus with Mohammed, Salaura and her band, which is associated with perfection and a legion of saints, are honored with the privilege of destroying the wolf, whom Nivardus clearly despised; and being represented by a sow (a creature normally disgusting to the author, as indicated by Ysengrimus's curse) fits the generally grotesque, ironic tone of the whole epic. We have learned that Reinardus also speaks for Nivardus once in a while, without always being his surrogate, as the Sprotinus episode shows. Both Salaura and the fox are treated ambivalently.

Looking back over *Ysengrimus* with the "abbess's" lamentation in mind, we can perceive that in essence it is a blackly humorous portrayal of this dog-eat-dog jungle which God is about to purge. Greed is viewed as our greatest sin, in accordance with 1 Timothy 6:10, which reads, "Cupidity is the root of all evils."[50] Nivardus wrote about animals in order to stress the beastliness of men. He made the wolf his protagonist because of that creature's notorious voracity. He made his protagonist a monk because he objected to avarice most in those who ought to be least tainted by it but were not. According to Ysengrimus in the latter half of the monastery episode (lines 1005–12 of Book V), the regular clergy were even more covetous than their secular breathren. The Sprotinus affair is included to show that greed is not limited to priests but also poisons laymen, like Reinardus, and the arrogant stork indicates that it can be desire for psychological, as well as material, aggrandizement. Egotism is a kind of avarice.[51] By being another wolf, the wife of Ysengrimus shares his appetence in general, but we see her ravenous for revenge. To Nivardus cupidity in almost any form, or hunger for whatever is ungodly, is the disease from which we are spiritually dying.

Evidently it is something he thought not only evil but also stupid, moreover, consonant with a tradition of construing faults as fatuous that dates from both classical and Hebraic antiquity. "Greed and good judgment can't mix," the fox observes in line 309 of Book VI. The insatiable wolf is a dunce, and sly Reinardus even plays the fool himself when hankering after Sprotinus. Jauss asserts that a contrast between wisdom and folly is *Ysengrimus*'s main motif, unifying all its episodes.[52] Though such an ethically neutral antithesis does indeed pervade the work, it is not so fundamental as Jauss contends. The most basic element is the moral issue of avarice, in keeping with Salaura's sermon and her victim's nature. (Not for nothing, after all, is the principal character a wolf—rather than an ass, for example, like Brunellus in Nigel's *Speculum Stultorum* of 1179–80.) More than anything else, cupidity makes a whole of all this epic's parts. For Nivardus it is normally the cause of foolishness and never the effect.

As a fresh historical example of how injurious it is, Salaura blames Pope Eugenius III (1145–53) for the failure of the Second Crusade, which was launched in 1147. She accuses him, though quite incorrectly, of having been bribed by Roger of Sicily to send the crusaders through Greece, where they were decimated, instead of through Italy. As a result, she says, both France and Germany have been ruined. Reinardus quips that His Holiness is trying to gather all the money in the world so that people will not sin by cutting up coins. *Ysengrimus* concludes with the fox purporting to wish that his enemy were still alive, to punish Salaura for maligning the pope. It is fitting that the end should be ironic, spoken by Reinardus, and concerned with greed and the wolf.

Nivardus basically created his final episode by combining two sources. One is the legend of Mohammed's death, probably as recorded by Embricho of Mainz in his poem of 571 distichs, *Vita Mahumeti,* from the first half of the eleventh century.[53] The second source survives in Marie de France's ninety-third fable, which deals with a wolf and a goat.[54] When the two chance to meet, the goat asks to say a Mass for the wolf and one for himself atop a nearby hill before he is eaten. All the animals who hear him, he states, will pray for them. His wish is granted, but his wail brings men on the run, who maul the wolf with their dogs. This story seems to have derived from a Greek fable in which a stray kid persuades a wolf to pipe while he dances, in order not to die disgracefully. Dogs hear the music and chase the wolf away.[55] Obviously Salaura behaves much like Marie's goat, so that the tradition in *Ysengrimus* scholarship of describing her clash with the wolf as Nivardus's original invention has been somewhat incorrect. Van Geertsom's idea that Salaura parodies Roland summoning Charlemagne is arresting but improbable, since the similarity is slight and Nivardus had no reason to travesty the *Chanson de Roland.*[56]

Although it is wordy, bizarre, and soured by its doomsday pessimism, which finds no good in life and overstates part of the bad, *Ysengrimus* does possess interesting subtleties, and it is often funny. Readers who can appreciate its Latin style will find it brilliantly written, if sometimes obscure. It deserves continuing study, but its importance will always tend to be historical rather than intrinsic. Whatever its inherent merits, it is valuable primarily because of Nivardus's leadership in the genre of the animal epic and his consequent influence on vernacular Reynard poems— to which we now turn.

Chapter Two

Early *Branches* of the *Roman de Renart*

About the year 1176 a trouvère named Pierre de Saint-Cloud wrote what seems to be the first medieval beast epic in a popular language.[1] It consists of some 2,410 eight-syllable verses in rhymed couplets, and its plot is devoted principally to another feud between the fox, named Renart, and Ysengrin the wolf, both of whom are barons in Noble the lion's kingdom. It was so well received that imitations soon appeared. By circa 1250 some twenty-six Gallic tales about Reynard (the exact number depending on how one counts) were circulating as so-called *branches*, in the same verse form as Pierre de Saint-Cloud's poem, and were being collected as the *Roman de Renart*. Initially the public may have referred to Pierre's novelty as the "Romance of Reynard," and the poets who first followed his example possibly thought of their creations as offshoots from that trunk. If so, the title nevertheless soon became generic, while *branche* was kept as the technical term for a Reynard epic in French.

Extant manuscripts of the *Roman de Renart* do not preserve its *branches* in any meaningful order. They deny Pierre's pioneering venture due prominence, for example, and even break it up most ignominiously. Standard numbering of the *Roman*'s *branches* today still reflects that confusion, despite the chronology established by Foulet.[2] Those poems are usually identified according to their order in Ernst Martin's edition of 1882–87,[3] which does not improve on the manuscripts. Pierre's original is known as *Branches* II and Va combined, and what is termed *Branche* I was not produced until after II-Va, III, IV, and XIV were already in existence (circa 1179).

Branches XV and V (which share the curious fate of having been joined to parts of II-Va)[4] probably also antedate I, though we cannot be sure that they do. There are allusions in I to II-Va, III, IV, and XIV but not so definitely to XV and V, while XV failed to influence the Middle-High-German epic *Reinhart Fuchs,* which was written during the 1190s and combines material from *Branches* I, II-Va, III, IV, V, VI, X, and maybe VIII. *Branche* V seems to anticipate XIV, however, and to be indebted to XV in turn. Because XV refers only to II-Va and III for certain, we will place it chronologically right after III, with V immediately following IV. The *branches* concerning us in this chapter are therefore II-Va, III, XV, IV, V, XIV, and I, in that presumptive order of composition. Among all the *Roman de Renart's branches* only II-Va and I are major works, but tracing the likely development of the beast epic from II-Va to I is an interesting part of our whole endeavor.

We will utilize Martin's edition rather than more recent ones, since it seems closest to the original version of each *branche* which we want to study.[5]

Branche II-Va

Whereas Nivardus composed *Ysengrimus*, with its difficult Latin, inverted structure, and comments on ecclesiastical personages, to be read by educated clerics, Pierre de Saint-Cloud wrote for recitation to lay nobility, addressed at the very beginning of his poem as *seigneurs.*

In a twenty-two-line prologue he asserts that he is breaking new ground, and he indicates that *Ysengrimus* was unknown to the general public. To familiar stories like those about Paris and Helen or Tristan, he declares, he will add an account of Renart's vendetta with Ysengrin, about which his audience has never heard. Because he ends his prologue by telling us to listen to what brought about the two barons' feud, we expect his work to open with the casus belli or at least with some background history, but we find that the first 1,000 lines contain only a series of episodes involving Renart's attempt to prey upon the rooster Chantecler, upon an unnamed titmouse, and upon Tiecelin the crow, as well as to injure the wildcat Tibert. Those verses do not at all deal with reasons for a war against the wolf.

As Foulet has pointed out,[6] Pierre was evidently influenced by Bruno the bear's poem in *Ysengrimus*, which relates how Reinardus endangered Sprotinus the cock and then befouled the wolf cubs. Pierre composed his narrative by building onto each of those disparate incidents, for he wanted to portray more than just a feud, despite not saying so in his prologue. We will see that what he created is in fact a satire on the seamy side of knighthood, so that the two major parts of his work are thematically related.

Whereas Nivardus identifies Reinardus right away as a fox, Pierre does not explain who Renart is, implying that in the folklore of northern France the fox had become better known during the generation since *Ysengrimus* appeared. The gentlemen for whom Pierre wrote seem to have been acquainted in advance with both Ysengrin and Renart, though not with a conflict between them. In contrast to that pair, all other named animals are carefully introduced. Because they are, Pierre should probably be credited with having christened most of them himself, following Nivardus's example. Only in regard to the fox, the wolf, and Brun the bear was he clearly not original.

Branche II, Verses 23–1026.   Altering Sprotinus's seduction and escape, Pierre handled in his own way the first episode which he borrowed from Nivardus. The French version appears to begin on a morning in July.[7] Renart, characterized as a master of devilish deceit, dives through the palisade around Constant des Noes's garden, landing among cabbage plants that conceal him. Constant's hens, who see something sail through the air, run for their roost, but Chantecler is sure that all of them are safe. So convinced is he that he acts like a fool, says Pierre (line 121), for he goes to sleep on a manure pile. He even dismisses a dream which his favorite wife Pinte interprets as a warning that before noon a fox will seize him by the throat.

During the second nap Renart lunges at him but misses out of impetuosity. To prevent him from flying away, the fox pretends that no harm is meant because the two are cousins. A resultant cry of relief inspires Renart to claim that the song of Chantecler's

father, who crowed with his eyes shut, could be heard for a
league, and the fox declares that losing a foot would be better
than hurting a relative. What Renart does not intend to be a
two-step process becomes one, as in *Ysengrimus*, for the cock
initially preserves sufficient caution merely to wink. When he
is persuaded to close both eyes, his beguiler grips him by the
neck and prances off.

In order for Chantecler's plight to be discovered, Pierre has
the time suddenly become evening (line 371), even though Pinte's
prediction of an attack before noon (line 252) indicated that only
slightly earlier it was still morning. The sun has lurched, as in
Nivardus's fishing episode. Because of the late hour, at any rate,
a woman comes to put the chickens in their coop and espies the
rooster slung across his abductor's back. She cries for help, sending all the farm hands in pursuit, and Constant sics dogs on
Renart, who has managed to carry his booty back through the
palisade.

Chantecler grows clever in adversity, appealing to the fox's
pride just as the fox has appealed to his. Without telling Renart
to lay him down first, he maintains that Constant should be
taunted. Cooperatively the fox then barks, "In spite of you I'm
taking what is mine," permitting what he thought was his to
fly into an apple tree. He squats below on a dungheap by way
of showing that he has assumed the rooster's role as dupe. Like
his counterpart in several of the fables reviewed in connection
with the Sprotinus incident, he curses the mouth which opens
when it should be shut, while a wiser Chantecler curses the eye
which shuts when it should be open. Despite the latter's sneer
that Renart must move along to keep his fur intact, his pursuers
have vanished, as not only in *Ysengrimus* but also in *Gallus et
Vulpes* and Marie de France's *Esope*.

Rather than keep Chantecler in his remake of the Sprotinus
episode's second stage, Pierre substituted another bird, the titmouse. With a different prey the peace ploy stands a better chance
of succeeding. Pierre must have known either Marie's *Esope,* in
which her fable about the fox and the dove immediately follows
the one about the fox and the cock, or an earlier version of it,

but perhaps he considered the dove a less worthy match for Renart than the tit, whom Marie presents elsewhere as "very wise, perceptive, and sly."[8]

Still reproaching himself for his stupidity, Renart spots that bird near her nest in a hollow oak. He asks her to come down and greet him with a kiss, but instead of complying she scolds him for his deviousness. To put her off guard, he says very nearly what he told Chantecler, lying that he never dreamed of displeasing her and reminding her that he is her son's godfather. He justifies his demand for a peck by claiming that King Noble has suspended all hostilities, to everyone's relief, though rather than wave a piece of birch bark in specious confirmation, like Reinardus, he encourages the tit to kiss him by promising to close his eyes.

She purports to acquiesce, but only in order to tease him. While he squints, she brushes his whiskers with leaves and moss. Of course he snaps, and she chides him for nearly breaking the putative law he has just cited. Excusing himself with the assertion that he was only joking, he urges her to kiss him again, just as he twice coaxed Chantecler to crow with eyes closed. The tit darts past his jaws, but too quickly to be caught. When Renart tries to elicit a third kiss, "in the name of holy charity," he gets no response at all. The stalemate that has developed is ended—not, as in *Ysengrimus* or *Esope,* by the bird professing to see hunters approach—but by a group of riders who really do intervene with their dogs, forcing Renart to search elsewhere for dinner, while the titmouse jeers.

So far in this escapade Pierre has combined three motifs, adding to the truce idea the complementary concepts of osculation and nictitation. The kiss's likeliest source is the Salaura episode of *Ysengrimus*, where bussing is also sought in the name of peace and where it is only a euphemism for biting. Foulet argues reasonably that closing the eyes is a carry-over from the Chantecler adventure.[9] Besides mingling several borrowed motifs in this episode, Pierre also extended it by annexing a subordinate affair apparently of his own invention.

Running down a path, Renart meets a lay brother with two bloodhounds on a leash. Such a pious gentleman should be fair and not interfere with the race in progress, the fox requests, for its stakes are high. Moved by Renart's eloquence, the lay brother turns away, commending to God and Saint Julian what would have made a splendid trophy. By galloping as if on horseback the fox outdistances his pursuers, who were stopped mysteriously while he conversed, reminding us of the peasants in Nivardus's fishing fiasco.

Tibert the cat approaches, twirling along as he chases his tail. Renart pretends to be at war with Ysengrin already and asks the bearer of sharp claws to join his mercenary army. Tibert consents, having a bone to pick with the wolf himself, and pledges his loyalty. Soon the perfidious fox attempts to lure him into a trap beside their trail by facetiously asking for a sample of his "equitation." Though neither of them is actually mounted, Renart requires the cat to demonstrate a make-believe charger. Tibert humors the fox by acting as if he were riding, but he discovers the trap in time to dodge it.

While the cat is dashing back and forth, on orders from his commander, two mastiffs burst into sight, just as other dogs terminated Renart's mischief with the tit. The fox's retreat on this occasion is less felicitous, however, because Tibert pushes him so that he steps into the trap himself, as he flees past it with the cat, and in place of an obliging lay brother he is confronted by the owner of the two mastiffs—a peasant with an ax. Tibert bounds away, scoffing like the cock and the tit. The peasant swings the ax but misses, smashing the trap and releasing Renart, who outruns the dogs despite having been injured. Though his foot was not cut off, we are still reminded of Nivardus's wolf on the frozen pond.

The affair with Tibert differs in a couple of ways from the adventures with Chantecler and the titmouse, as well as from the contest with Tiecelin, which follows. All three of those episodes have known antecedents, while the Tibert incident does not. It was probably invented by Pierre, like the brush with the lay brother. The other three encounters are also attempts at fowling for the sake of food, whereas with the cat Renart is only proving how gratuitously malicious he can be.

The dialog with Tiecelin the crow is carefully placed in a *locus amoenus,* which augurs a happy end. While the fox reclines on grass beneath a beech tree, near a river between two mountains, Sir Tiecelin lights on a limb above him, successfully completing what Pierre portrays as a knightly adventure. The crow has stolen a cheese. Instead of holding it in his beak, like his counterpart in such fables as Marie de France's thirteenth, [10] he presses it between his feet and pecks at it. This procedure is more practical and also permits a dramatic crescendo, since Tiecelin can talk without at once dropping his prize. Alerted by a falling crumb, Renard eulogizes the crow's late father Rohart, "who knew how to warble so well." To prove that he too can sing, Tiecelin curdles the air with his sour croak, which the fox sweetly praises. This routine is twice repeated, the raucous caw growing louder and shriller each time, until with the strain the cheese is released. Thus Pierre has Renart reuse the technique which proved effective with Chantecler[11] rather than compliment Tiecelin on his beauty and wish that his song were comparable.

Fox-crow fables regularly conclude when such cajolery pays off, but Pierre decided to append a second act to his version of the little farce, in order to impress on us Renart's (and many a cavalier's) wicked cunning. Just as he sought to murder Chantecler and the tit and at least to hurt the cat, so Renart now has designs on the life of Tiecelin. Rather than gobble up the redolent cheese, he spurns it as if it were nauseous. Exposing his damaged foot, much as foxes in bestiaries trick crows by playing dead, he whines that strong odors are bad for cripples. Tiecelin believes him and hops down, having not yet eaten enough. As with the rooster, Renart's inevitable pounce goes awry, leaving him with only a mouthful of feathers. He wants to soothe the crow as he soothed the cock, but Tiecelin flutters away. The episode, and thus the whole series of episodes, concludes with Renart being forced to dine less harmfully than intended.

Although the four little dramas are not a part of the feud which Pierre heralds in his prologue and they even lack unity among

themselves, on account of the lay brother and Tibert, Pierre must
have included them not just to introduce the fox, as Foulet
surmises, [12] but to caricature various types of unworthy knights—
complacent ones, like Chantecler; thieving ones, like the crow;
and deceitful, vicious ones, like Renart, who did not even scruple
to scheme against allies and ladies. Surely the fox's failure in each
of these early capers reflects his author's disapproval of him. His
acquisition of the cheese is not so much his reward as Tiecelin's
punishment, and it is more than offset by his wounded foot.
(Lameness serves him right especially on account of his assertion
that he would rather be a cripple than harm Chantecler.) Pierre
was most concerned about the causes and conduct of feuds, however. Not only does his prologue indicate that he was; he also
devoted the greater part of his poem to Ysengrin's struggle with
Renart. In doing so he no longer strung episodes together like
Nivardus but rather told a single, continuous story. Though it
has different stages, the one underlying conflict throughout is
between the fox and the wolf.

   Branche II, Verses 1027–1392, and *Branche* Va, Verses
257–1272.   After nourishing himself with the cheese, Renart
roams about and chances upon a cave. In a parenthetical comment
the author informs us that the long-awaited fray with "Constable
Ysengrin" is about to begin. Nivardus's unfrocked monk has
been promoted to high officialdom, like the earlier wolf in *Ecbasis
Captivi* or as in Marie de France's sixty-eighth fable. (See the sick-
lion episode in Chapter One.)[13] Pierre had no use for a mindless
embodiment of clerical rapacity, and he wanted the fox's foe to
be politically powerful, for a reason that will become apparent
near the end of the epic.

   Not until Renart enters the cave does he realize that it is
Ysengrin's abode. The master is out on the prowl, but the mistress
Hersent is nursing four cubs. She jumps up, reproaching her
guest for his unsociableness in not having visited her sooner.
Renart apologizes by explaining that her husband hates him in
the belief that he loves her. Thus the fox and the wolf are at odds
here not, as in *Ysengrimus,* on account of the universal threat
posed by lupine gluttony but rather because Ysengrin fears being

cuckolded. Treated as a rival, Renart reacts as one, especially now that Hersent encourages him. She makes her spouse's jealousy the grounds for a real affair, since unlike her equivalent in Nivardus's epic she is too lascivious to be faithful. She is what Ysengrimus's loyal wife became in the interpolation at the end of Nivardus's wolf-den episode, giving Ysengrin good reason to be suspicious. In a parody of courtly love à la *Tristan* she asks the red knight to kiss her, and the couple embrace.

Before departing, Renart also takes advantage of the chance to gorge himself at his adversary's expense and to mistreat the latter's offspring. In effect he declares war by sprinkling the whelps with his urine, throwing them from their bed, and calling them bastards. As though she despised them too, Hersent does not interfere. Insead of chasing the fox, she even pleads with her young not to inform their father. They tell him everything when he returns, however, and he furiously berates his wife. She placates him by offering to vindicate herself with a test of her innocence, by pledging him total obedience, and by vowing to kill Renart if she ever can. At this point the sun, which was already sinking low more than 800 lines earlier, is finally allowed to set.

Several days later the two wolves chance upon the fox and run after him as he figuratively "spurs" for home. Ysengrin falls behind, leaving Hersent to pursue vengeance alone. When she reaches Renart's den, called Valcrues,[14] she tries to ram herself through its narrow entrance, like her counterpart at Reinardus's burrow in *Ysengrimus,* and becomes stuck. She is also raped, although the fox knows that her mate is looking for him. He may be motivated less by lust than by malice, and he does not stop belaboring Hersent until he is discovered at work. In typically two-faced fashion he denies the obvious, however, insisting to Ysengrin, who is still at a distance, that he has only been trying to dislodge the impetuous lady. He offers to swear formally that he is above reproach, for he fears God no more than the wolf. After he has withdrawn, Ysengrin concludes *Branche* II by digging Hersent loose.

Her efforts to please her husband have backfired. He is as angry at her as he was in their cave, when the story is resumed in

Branche Va. She calms him down this time by pointing out that she has obviously been abused, and he welcomes her proposal that they complain of the assault at Noble's court, to which they make their way at once. Since Renart has committed a crime, the shortest route to revenge could be the one to the royal throne. The wolves' decision seems reasonable, and it is indeed logic more than *Ysengrimus*'s influence that determines how the plot unfolds from this point on.

Because of his position, his smartness, and his learning (he knows several languages) Ysengrin is likely to win out over Renart provided he can bring the latter to trial, Pierre remarks (lines 292–98). Even though we may be surprised to see intelligence attributed to the wolf, the author is not ironic here, since Ysengrin definitely does have rank. The comment helps reveal, instead, to what extent Nivardus's dolt has been altered.

When the wolf couple enter Noble's palace (or tent, according to line 506), they find all manner of subjects there, with the sovereign's suite in a circle around him. Everyone is silent. Ysengrin steps forward and charges Renart with having broken an imperial law safeguarding marriage, as Hersent can confirm. She testifies that since she was a girl Renart has hounded her, finally possessing her against her will. Ysengrin, who reports having observed the outrage, adds an account of what its perpetrator also did to his children and concludes with a reference to the oath which Renart volunteered to swear.

Averse to chastising a gentleman for an amour, despite the law against adultery, Noble impugns the she-wolf's credibility until her mate objects, whereupon he seeks advice from one Musart, a Lombard camel. This droll creature is a papal legate visiting the lion's court (and the caricature of an actual legate, Pietro di Pavia, in France from 1174 to 1178).[15] Surely with tongue in cheek now, since *musart* means "foolish," Pierre terms the camel "very wise and a good jurist." In pidgin French flavored with Italian and Latin Musart proclaims that the fox must be severely punished if not exonerated; but Noble hints, when calling for a verdict from his barons, that Renart should be pardoned for gallantry.

Pierre informs us that "more than a thousand" courtiers huddled to argue the fox's case. We hear from only Brichemer the stag (Noble's seneschal), Brun the bear, Baucent the boar, Plateax the fallow deer, and the monkey Cointereax, however. While sympathizing with Ysengrin, Brichemer goes objectively and at once to the heart of the matter—the absence of a reliable witness, since a spouse's testimony is suspect—only to be contradicted by Brun, who contends that the constable is too eminent to be doubted. Baucent sides with the stag, while Plateax seconds the bear.

In an effort to support the wolves, Brun relates in a 141-line digression how he himself was victimized not long ago, Renart having duped him into believing that he would find honey at Constant des Noes's farm when in reality he only served to decoy both men and dogs, who nearly killed him, while the fox abducted a chicken unscathed. Brun also reports that Tiecelin, Tibert, and the tit have recently lodged complaints against Renart. Returning to the present situation, Baucent, endorsed by Cointereax, maintains that standard procedure demands an examination of the defendant. Again Brun prolongs the debate, insisting that justice be short-circuited and the accused, against whom he is biased, be summarily treated as a convicted adulterer. Pierre's attention to the bear's lynch mentality implies that it was of topical importance, but a modern reader is likely to sigh with relief over Brichemer's resolution of the 360-line controversy. What the stag proposes, winning the court's approval (though surely not the wolves') is that Renart should swear his oath of innocence. Since Noble is about to leave the country, the universally respected mastiff Roonel should officiate at the ceremony, to be held the following Sunday.

His Majesty happily sanctions this compromise and dispatches Grimbert the badger to apprise Renart, the two being kinsmen. [16] With court adjourned, Grimbert travels straightway to the fox's residence, which is now called either Malpertuis, Valpertuis, or Malcrues, depending on the manuscript. [17] Renart concurs, intending to perjure himself, but Ysengrin takes steps to overtrump him.

The constable visits Roonel, requesting that this court-appointed judge side with him. Despite having been portrayed by Brichemer as a paragon of virtue, Roonel suggests a particularly impious way of tricking Renart. Since the latter is to swear on a holy relic, the mastiff will pretend to have died; Renart can be asked to sanctify his oath by touching the open jaws of this "saintly" personage. Of course they will snap shut, like the trap in the perjury episode of *Ysengrimus*. Ironically, Roonel will be borrowing the vulpine ruse which Renart varied with Tiecelin and subjecting the fox to what Reinardus brought upon the wolf in Nivardus's poem. Should Renart balk, a small army of other dogs will be lurking in ambush. Not yet content, however, Ysengrin recruits more supporters, including Brichemer, Baucent, and Cointereax, who thus abandon their prior impartiality. In the France of his day, Pierre wanted to say, equity was undermined by politics. The wolf has become a dignitary in order to possess enough influence for that point to be made. He cannot obtain an improper verdict, but he can subvert the verdict which he does obtain. Musart sides with him, and Noble sends him a personal deputy, the leopard, while Tibert, once an opponent of the wolf, understandably joins Ysengrin's party now. Renart is not without allies, too, his principal backer being Grimbert.

At the appointed time both factions come to where the mastiff is playing possum, sprawled on his back with fangs bared. Hidden in a nearby orchard are more than a hundred canine cronies, thirsting for fox blood. Brichemer instructs Renart to acquit himself by proclaiming, with his right hand on Roonel's teeth, that he has been falsely accused. At this climactic moment the fox detects the "corpse's" breathing and steps back. Grimbert, who has also noticed Roonel's ruse, asserts that the crowd is pressing too close. When Brichemer has everyone make room, Renart decamps.

The dogs from the orchard race after him, parodying knightly chases and terminating the conflict with Ysengrin in much the same fashion as the designs on Chantecler, the titmouse, and Tibert were concluded. Pierre spends the last eighty-eight lines of his poem identifying seventy-eight of the pursuers and describing how they nipped the fox's fur before he reached home (Malpertuis). As if everyone were mounted, the leader of the pack, Roonel, is said to carry a lance. Bleeding in more than thirteen places, the scoundrel Renart escapes death but not vengeance, so that a moral of "crime does not pay" can be inferred. Both in the first 1,000 lines of the story and in the last 1,400 he neither fails nor succeeds completely. More sinned against than sinning as regards the fox, Ysengrin ultimately seeks justice in an unjust way, making it appropriate that he settle for less than he likes.

Pierre burlesques deceit, violence, and corruption on the part of supposedly noble knights. All too often, he hints, they behaved like animals, especially when feuding. Some of them were not above rape and the abuse of children in their belligerence, which was frequently occasioned by a woman (like the Trojan War, referred to in the prologue).[18] Even society's pillars might lean toward one of their number when he himself ethically sagged. Albeit inspired by *Ysengrimus,* Pierre was not preoccupied with greed, and he was in no way critical of the clergy. He lampooned Pietro di Pavia because he objected to that dignitary as a person and a lawyer[19] rather than as an ecclesiastic. Musart's religiousness is never impugned. It was the secular elite—the kind of men who must have listened to his poem—that Pierre took obliquely and facetiously to task.

Another facet of *Ysengrimus* which he forsook, perhaps because his plot compelled him to drop it, is Reinardus's role as the wolf's invidious adviser. Brun's account of how Renart misled him once is the only instance in II-Va of malign counsel by the fox. Renart does not really give advice even to Tibert, while he has no occasion to urge a course of action on Ysengrin. The relationship between fox and wolf established by Nivardus was implicitly restored in *Branches* III, IV, XIV, and I (Renart's confession), and it was made explicit again in *Branche* V, as we will see.

That Pierre bestowed more attention on Renart than on Ysengrin overall did not result from a preference for the former but, on the contrary, from aversion to the combination of duplicity and viciousness which characterizes a fox better than a wolf.

Renart may not have been more popular than Ysengrin before
1176, though most of Pierre's imitators certainly did favor the
fox, probably on account of his prominence in the first 1,000
lines of *Branche* II-Va and also because a wolf is not supposed to
be so capable and clever.

Branche III

In what must have been a very short time after Pierre's epic
became known, an anonymous minstrel composed 510-line
Branche III. The fact that III resembles II-Va in containing no
allusions to any other *branche* suggests that it was produced quite
early, yet Pierre's prologue indicates that his work still takes
precedence chronologically. In III the fox also starts a feud with
the wolf, moreover, so that Pierre could not have made his claim
to "originality" if III antedated II-Va.

Like him, the author of III begins by addressing an audience
as *seigneurs,* but in contrast to Pierre he wanted to entertain rather
than to satirize. Another difference is that no prologue follows
in III, just as there is none in *Ysengrimus.* We are plunged immediately into the narrative by being informed that the season
is winter. More precisely, we are later told, it is shortly before
Christmas. As hungry as at the outset of II-Va, Renart leaves his
now nameless burrow and hunts for food. In the first two of the
branche's three episodes (though only for the sake of the second)
the den is said to be a castle with windows and a door that opens
and closes.[20]

As he lurks beside a road, the fox sees a couple of fish merchants
driving their wagon toward him. He plays dead, better than
Roonel in II-Va, and for the sake of his pelt the two men toss
him atop their load. While they travel on, he gobbles over thirty
herring and wreathes himself with eels. His astonished benefactors
chase him when he bids them adieu, but he has too fast a horse,
as the author jokes in line 141.

One of that poet's major innovations is to have blessed the fox
with a family. Although Reinardus indicates that he has cubs in
the wolf-den episode of *Ysengrimus,*[21] we never see them or hear
of them again, and his wife is not even mentioned. Pierre de

Saint-Cloud drops no hint that Renart has either a mate or off-spring in II-Va, but in III we find him married to gentle Herme-line, who has borne him two sons, Percehaie and Malebranche. The three of them welcome him heartily, and not just because of his viands, though they quickly prepare the eels for roasting.

Their supper's aroma reaches the nostrils of half-starved Ysen-grin, who in his stupid voraciousness is much more Nivardus's wolf than Pierre's. He squats outside a window to the fox's res-idence and howls for its door to be opened, but Renart, who pretends that the building is a cloister belonging to the order of Tiron (which actually existed), refuses to admit a layman. *"No-mini dame!"* Ysengrin exclaims, introducing into vernacular Rey-nard epics the use of comically corrupt Latin, reminiscent of *cominus ovis cum* in the monastery episode of *Ysengrimus.* When the wolf asks what the brothers are eating, Renart alleges that they always dine on seafood (and the Tiron monks did).[22] He extends a sample, expressing the hope that Ysengrin will join their congregation. Just for being tonsured the wolf can consume any amount of fish, Renart affirms. Naturally Ysengrin consents, so the fox has him stick his head inside and pours boiling water over it.

In addition Renart stipulates that the "novice" must be tested for a night, by catching fish for the "abbey." He leads Ysengrin to a frozen pond, where there is still a hole in the ice cut by farmers for their cattle. The wolf sits there till dawn, with a bucket tied to his tail. Renart does not have to lure a mob to the scene, because a vavasor named Constant des Granches (after Pierre's peasant Constant des Noes) comes hunting with his men. Drawing a sword, the chasseur tries to accomplish what Aldrada sought in *Ysengrimus,* yet he also misses twice, whacking the fisher's tail in two on his second attempt. After fighting off the hunters' dogs and escaping, Ysengrin ends *Branche* III by vowing enmity against Renart, who has meanwhile returned to his home, now called a den (line 445).

Ysengrimus probably inspired both the second and third episodes of this poem, as Foulet has argued,[23] but whereas Nivardus in-cluded a sham ordainment primarily so that monks in general might be satirized by means of his wolf, the author of *Branche* III saw Ysengrin's induction into a putative cloister as merely an excuse for twofold torture (through both tonsuring and testing). While Renart, like Reinardus, entices the wolf into monasticism for the sake of food, moreover, the author of *Branche* III changed the kind of food initially proffered. Instead of cakes he has his fox bait Ysengrin with eels, in anticipation of the fishing affair and in accordance with medieval folklore, which often combined the first caper with the trick on the frozen pond.[24] Although *Branche* III is episodic, it is unified both by the importance of fish throughout and also by the fact that the third adventure develops from the second and the second from the first. The Tiron order's ban on meat, making the order apropos, is probably why Renart identifies with it.

Branche XV

Consisting of two episodes rather than three, 522-line *Branche* XV is also well integrated. Its pair of tales resemble each other to some extent, sharing the same moral. They also share one of the same characters, but he is Tibert rather than Renart. Even though Ysengrin is totally absent, the unknown author ridicules greed, like Nivardus, particularly on the part of clergymen. His first anecdote, involving Tibert, Renart, and a sausage, is varied in the second, where two priests replace the fox and the cat. Tibert then partly functions like the sausage, which has been appropriately eliminated because the cat himself has eaten it. The avarice of both Renart and Rufrangier, the fox's substitute in the later episode, is punished by Tibert, with the priest being chastised worse, since his is the greater sin. Probably no accident in this thoughtfully constructed piece is the alliteration linking Renart to his equivalent, while Torgis is the name of the cat's counterpart.

Without any prologue we are informed that the treacherous fox sets out to appease his hunger. Though Pierre de Saint-Cloud does not indicate that Renart would eat Tibert in *Branche* II-Va, the author of XV states that the fox is eager to devour the cat, so famished is he, when he meets Tibert again. He also wants revenge for what happened in II-Va. To put his quarry off guard, he acts friendly, telling the cat not to run away but to honor the pledge of assistance made in Pierre's poem. Tibert remains, monitorially sharpening his claws, and for thirty-nine lines he is lectured on selfishness. Like Ysengrin, who recently became a monk, says Renart in an illusion to *Branche* III, everyone seeks his own advantage at others' expense, but malice will backfire. For that reason he does not want to be false, the fox alleges falsely. It was egotistic of Tibert to abandon him before, Renart continues, referring once more to their encounter in II-Va, but he pretends that the cat must still have been distressed over his peril. He concludes his sermon by relating that the peasant missed him. With a show of good will on both sides, the fox and Tibert restore their previous relationship, vowing mutual loyalty, but the author warns that it will not be of much duration.

Indeed, the pair soon find a long sausage, which Renart is unwilling to share, despite his championship of altruism. As he carries it in his mouth, dragging each end on the ground, the cat protests that he is spoiling it. Tibert offers to demonstrate a proper manner of conveyance, and the fox acquiesces, thinking that he can overpower his partner when the latter is encumbered. Seizing one tip of the sausage and tossing the rest across his back (the way Renart shoulders Chantecler in II-Va), the cat declares that they will be safe on a nearby hill, where a tall cross stands. There they can see whoever approaches. The fox, who wanted to seduce Tibert, is hoist by his own petard in accordance with his speech on perfidy, for the cat dashes ahead and scampers up the cross, on an arm of which he eats the meat. All in all, therefore, Tibert essentially repeats his role at the trap in II-Va, though the fox has a different part to play on this occasion. He essentially repeats his role at the foot of the oak tree in Pierre's titmouse episode, since he is teased at length. Ultimately he is even forced away by a hunter with dogs. A feud, observes the author, has now commenced between Renart and Tibert.

After the fox has been removed, Rufrangier and Torgis ride toward the cross on their way to a synod. Discovering Tibert still perched on high, they long for his pelt, much as the two fish

mongers crave Renart's in *Branche* III. Rufrangier, who dreams
of a cat-skin hat, consents to pay Torgis one-half of Tibert's
appraised value. Ignoring the cross's symbolism in his avarice,
he stands on his horse in order to reach the cat, who slaps him
to the ground with those claws which threatened Renart. Tibert
then leaps onto the empty saddle and is whisked to Rufrangier's
house. When he arrives, his galloping palfrey bowls over the
priest's concubine, so that she is punished in roughly the same
fashion as her lover. He suffers more, however, for he is scratched
as well as felled, and he hits his head when he lands, nearly
braining himself. Instead of proceeding to his conference, he goes
back home, convinced that a devil has hexed him.

Branche IV

This little work in 478 verses has a thirty-two-line prologue
in which a nameless minstrel tells his listeners that he is going
to amuse them with a *branche* (and he uses that word) comprising
a single anecdote about the fox. To arouse our curiosity and
maybe also to incline us toward accepting what will happen to
Renart, the author concludes his introduction with a proverb
cited by both Nivardus and Pierre de Saint-Cloud when their
roosters trick their foxes: "No one on earth is so wise as not to
be sometimes a fool."

If the anecdote is single, it still has two main parts (like
Branches II-Va and XV), and they can be further divided. The
first principal section, inspired by Pierre's Chantecler episode,
sets up the second, in which Renart blunders by riding a bucket
to the bottom of a well like Brer Rabbit in *Uncle Remus*. As we
will see, however, he does not do so for the same reason as Brer
Rabbit, who seeks a cool respite from hot summer work. His
motive is also different from his counterpart's in the fable which
must have served as the source for the second half of *Branche* IV.[25]
Chapter 23 of Petrus Alphonsi's early twelfth-century storybook
Disciplina Clericalis is about a fox taking a wolf at night to a well
in which the full moon is mirrored. Believing this reflection to
be a cheese the fox has promised him, the wolf orders the fox to
bring it up, though he offers to help if needed. The fox descends

in a bucket and claims that the cheese is too big for him, so the wolf climbs into the other bucket, not realizing that when the second goes down the first will go up. Being lighter, the fox ascends, hops out, and leaves the wolf to thrash about in the water.

The plot of *Branche* IV begins one evening as Renart, again half starved, comes upon a Cistercian abbey, the barn of which houses delectable chickens. After leaping through the surrounding wall, he has second thoughts about risking his life any further, but hunger drives him on. He sneaks into the barn and kills three chickens, at once devouring two of them. The third he plans to take home and cook, though whether he ultimately does so the author neglects to state. [26] A comic touch is applied by portraying the chicken thief parodically as a knight attacking a castle, rather like the way Pierre handles Tiecelin's theft of the cheese. Renart is said to want to "joust," for example, and to be in danger because the monks might hold him for ransom. Thus, and not because he is actually on a horse, we are also told that he does not "rein in" until he reaches the chickens.

The whole point of the preliminary incident is to bring the fox into the monastery and make him thirsty enough to inspect its well before leaving. Aware that he cannot safely reach the water, he gazes at it sadly and discovers his reflection, even though no moon is mentioned, in contrast to the *Disciplina-Clericalis* story. Mistaking his image for his wife Hermeline, he asks what she is doing down there, and the echo strengthens his illusion. In order to check on the woman he loves, he descends in a bucket, no longer mindful of reality. His senses are restored as soon as he hits the bottom, but then he is trapped.

How can he become so foolish that he mistakes his echo and reflection for his wife? He is not Petrus Alphonsi's stupid wolf. Indeed, he is not just any fox. The prologue declares that he is the clever and wise Renart we have already come to know, and later references to events in *Branche* II-Va will certify that both he and Ysengrin are supposed to be the same figures portrayed by Pierre. The wolf is more the embodiment of appetite that we found in *Branche* III and *Ysengrimus,* however, while so far in

Branche IV Renart is too naive to have an antecedent in any of the works we have seen. Pierre's fox is tricked by Chantecler, the titmouse, and Tibert, but divine justice is on their side and they can be crafty, whereas a well is always simple.

The author of the variant in Manuscript H (note 26 to this chapter) must also have been unhappy with the fox's romantic delusion. He eliminated it, sending Renart into the depths only because the fox needs a drink after eating. Unfortunately, this simplification is also infelicitous, for it necessitates an ignorance of buckets on a pulley that is unlikely in a chicken thief accustomed to farms. (Brer Rabbit's misadventure suffers from the same sort of flaw.) After puzzling over the arrangement, the fox jumps into the pail at the top of the well, thinking it full, and vanishes down the shaft.

Returning to *Branche* IV's initial version, we find that before long Ysengrin explores the abbey in his own search for victuals and happens by the well. As he peers into it like Renart ahead of him, lines 155–58, which described how the fox hung on the edge, staring pensively down, are duplicated (lines 203–206), so that the parallelism in both actions is stressed.[27] In the manner of Renart, the wolf sees his reflection and assumes his spouse to be sojourning under ground, yet because he perceives the fox there, too, he infers that he is being cuckolded again, as in Pierre's classic, a knowledge of which the author of *Branche* IV (like XV's author) presupposed on the part of his audience.

No sooner does Renart speak up than Ysengrin forgets about Hersent and his reflection, however, for the fox professes to be in heaven, having died not long ago. He describes paradise as such a happy hunting ground—full of cattle, sheep, goats, and hares[28]—that the wolf wants access to it also, but Renart asserts that Ysengrin has been too wicked, making false accusations at court. The fox plays further with the wolf by telling him he must beg God to forgive his sins before being weighed in the balance (the buckets), so his good deeds will be heavier than the bad ones. Ysengrin, who says that he has already confessed to (i.e., consumed) a rabbit and a nanny goat, consequently genuflects and howls at his Maker, uncouthly pointing his rear toward the east just as his spiritual mentor has reversed the directions of heaven and hell in this sneer at religion.[29] Renart then refers to what are probably the reflections of stars and calls them candles burning on the water as a miraculous sign of Christ's forgiveness. The wolf jumps into the empty bucket and plummets down, while the fox rockets up. As they pass, Renart shouts that Ysengrin is really going to hell, not heaven. According to folklore, wells are indeed entrances to the underworld,[30] but the fox simply means that his foe is bound for bedevilment.

Some monks who attempt to draw water the next morning discover the bedraggled bather cowering in the lower bucket. They call for reinforcements, and every member of the fraternity arrives, armed with something.[31] Ysengrin is pummeled when hoisted aloft, though the abbot spares his life. In staggering away he meets one of his sons, who vows revenge not only for this atrocity but also for what Renart did previously in their home (during *Branche* II-Va). Ysengrin limps to the cave, where doctors restore him.

Branche V

Much like the concluding lines of *Branche* III, the last three verses in IV state that the wolf will avenge himself if he comes upon the fox. Those verses form a nice transition to 246-line *Branche* V, which consists of two main parts without a prologue. The first section is an abbreviated version of Nivardus's ham episode, and the second is a basically similar but otherwise unknown encounter between Renart and a cricket, abruptly terminated by an incursion of dogs.

When Renart meets the wolf one day, Ysengrin threatens to swallow him, ripping up his fur with much more violence than in the Latin source. Because the fox lies still, the wolf becomes alarmed at the possibility of having killed his "counselor," as he says, acknowledging that his relationship to Renart is the same as Ysengrimus's to Reinardus. He also resembles Nivardus's wolf by being the fox's uncle rather than merely Renart's godfather, as in most *branches* (though he is that, too).

Descrying a peasant with a ham, the fox proposes that they trick the man out of it. With a pretense of lameness he causes the rustic to pursue him, discarding the ham and stumbling far afield. By the time Renart returns, Ysengrin has downed all the meat, saving only the rope by which it hung. Instead of reproaching his perfidious uncle, Renart excuses himself to insure his safety, alleging that he must visit Santiago Compostella.

For two weeks he wanders around dressed as a pilgrim,[32] yet without the attitude of one, because he desires revenge. He also wants something to eat as he arrives at a priest's house teeming with rats. He is unable to catch any of them, but with a detachable sleeve he manages to bag a cricket chanting near an oven. Just as Reinardus behaves like Ysengrimus in regard to Sprotinus, so Renart behaves like Ysengrin here. Whereas Ysengrin seems not to have been serious about devouring Renart, however, Renart is quite serious about devouring the cricket. When the cricket (named Frobert by the author of *Branche* I)[33] objects that murder misbecomes a pilgrim, Renart avers that he merely wanted to ingest the caroler's psalter in order to know more hymns. Hoping to put his prey off guard with a pious pose, he pretends that he is about to expire and asks whether he might confess his sins to the cricket, since the priest at whose house they are is not around. "You're about to have plenty of 'priests,' " the cricket cries, hearing hunters with their dogs, which chase Renart until he eludes them by hiding atop the oven. As if God were heeding the fox's wish for vengeance, Ysengrin appears, and the dogs nip him much as he nipped Renart two weeks earlier.

Having flatly plagiarized Nivardus in his first episode, the author of *Branche* V was a less slavish imitator in his second incident, for it is essentially a recasting of the contest between Sprotinus and another would-be pilgrim who is also put to flight by dogs. Sprotinus's hounds are mere make-believe, but the effect is the same. (Although Foulet sees influence only from Pierre de Saint-Cloud in the second episode, he contends correctly that it manifests itself in the dogs' names.)[34] To tie the two incidents together, through a combination of elements from both, *Branche*

V's author added the coda in which Ysengrin is punished by Renart's pursuers.

The cricket's ironic reference to hunters as "priests" (lines 200–201) resembles a joke by Tibert in lines 314–24 of *Branche* XV. Probably inspired by the Salaura episode of *Ysengrimus*, the cat speaks there of invading dogs as "a company . . . celebrating mass and matins." The similarity between that jest and the cricket's in *Branche* V could be coincidental, but both structurally and thematically V mirrors XV, which likewise consists of two related episodes concerned with greed. The artistic superiority of XV, which is more imaginative than V, suggests that it was V's model rather than vice versa. The author of V took his structure from XV, his contents from *Ysengrimus*, and his theme from both. Foulet misjudged V in affirming that its creator did not follow ham dupery with ice fishing like Nivardus simply because *Branche* III was already in existence.[35]

Branche XIV

Like all preceding poems in the *Roman de Renart,* 1,088-line XIV opens with a hungry fox looking for food. The resemblance is greatest to III, for Renart is initially at his home (called Malpertuis), but the time is in May, near Ascension Day rather than Christmas. The action in XIV, as in IV, commences at night, though in neither work are we told so explicitly. Unlike IV, XIV has no prologue.

Near a farm belonging to a peasant named Gonbaut, Renart again meets Tibert, who wants some milk which Gonbaut's wife keeps in a bin. Together the cat and the fox find a hole in Gonbaut's palisade and proceed to the house, Renart agreeing to assist his companion before attacking any poultry, which might awaken Gonbaut's dogs. While Tibert laps contentedly, down inside the hutch, Renart obligingly strains to hold up its heavy lid. Not only does the cat take his time, but when he has drunk his fill he spills what is left of the milk to prevent the fox from enjoying any. In *Branches* XV and XIV together he therefore cheats Renart out of both food and drink, but in XIV the fox gets even, dropping the lid too soon and bobbing Tibert's tail when the cat finally jumps from the bin. By averring that the loss is really a gain, since Tibert will have less to lug around, Renart reminds us of Ysengrimus telling Corvigarus that the sacrifice of some flesh would help the horse to run faster.

At the chicken coop the fox accepts the cat's malicious advice to take the rooster rather than any of the hens because the latter are molting. When he has seized the cock, which is said to be perched next to Pinte, even though the flock belongs to Gonbaut instead of to Constant des Noes, Tibert asks him whether he is holding his prize securely. Renart repeats the old mistake of opening his mouth to reply. This time the cock not only escapes but also rouses Gonbaut by crowing. The farmer sets two dogs on the fox, who is roughed up and chased away. Tibert absconds ahead of him and will not be seen again in *Branche* XIV.

The enterprise of Renart and the cat to some extent resembles the fox's and Brun's as recounted by Pierre's bear at court. In each story Renart and a comrade sneak into a farm for their favorite food, but in *Branche* XIV the comrade succeeds, while the fox is attacked. Rather than exploit the cat like the bear, moreover, Renart is exploited himself, since he vainly props the lid.

Through the remaining 890 lines he plays a succession of five tricks on Ysengrin's brother Primaut, a character invented by XIV's author. Thus, as Foulet has pointed out,[36] the basic format of this poem seems to have been derived from Pierre's, where the fox warms up with several lightweight but agile sparring partners before his main bout with a ponderous wolf. There is no question of a single conflict between Primaut and Renart, however, and Primaut in his obtuse voracity apes the Ysengrin of *Branches* III, IV, and V or Nivardus's wolf much more than Pierre's. A fox giving a wolf misleading advice in a series of episodes is also reminiscent of *Ysengrimus*.

After outrunning Gonbaut's dogs, Renart discovers a box of hosts dropped by a tipsy priest. He eats all but two of them, and when he meets Primaut he gives the rest to the wolf, alleging that he found them in a nearby village church. Because Primaut wants more, Renart conducts him to that sanctuary, just as Reinardus lures Ysengrimus into Saint Peter's with cakes. By digging under the threshold, Renart and Primaut enter, finding not only more hosts but also meat, bread, and wine, hidden away by the same priest who lost the hosts outside and is therefore a gluttonous hamster as well as a drunk. In the course of banqueting, Primaut swills too much wine, like Ysengrimus in the monastery cellar, with the result that he wishes to hold a vesper service. The hour is not quite appropriate, but an alb, a chasuble, and a missal are lying on the altar. The author of *Branche* XIV was probably thinking of Ysengrimus's mock consecration as bishop, though Nivardus is less sacrilegious. The leering disrespect for religion in this episode also transcends what we found in *Branche* IV.

Foulet asserts that Ysengrin is replaced with Primaut primarily because he had become too well known as the fox's foe for Renart and him to consort as Renart and Primaut do here.[37] Being Reinardus's enemy does not prevent Ysengrimus from being duped repeatedly by Nivardus's fox, however. A better reason is that the author of XIV wanted a farcical tonsuring as a preliminary to burlesquing vespers, and Ysengrin had already received one in *Branche* III. He had no need for another. The depilation in XIV reflects that in III, where boiling water is poured over Ysengrin's head, because Renart shaves Primaut after dousing him with urine.

Feeling qualified to proceed with the service on account of his baldness, Primaut rings the church bells, dons the vestments, leafs through the missal, and howls, oblivious to danger and Renart, who slips out and packs shut their hole beneath the door. Awakened by the noise, the curé peeks through a crack and beholds the wolf, whose presence he announces to parishioners by shouting through the village streets. Everyone hops out of bed, arms himself, and batters the unwelcome worshiper, rather like Bovo's congregation in the fishing episode of *Ysengrimus*.

Renart has kept one herring for Primaut after fooling some merchants as in *Branche* III. Despite the feast in the church the wolf is still hungry enough to try the fox's ruse, when he rejoins Renart in the forest. Instead of being tossed aboard the fish cart, however, he is almost killed. Just in time to avoid being stabbed

with a sword, he jumps up and reels back to Renart, aching from
new blows.

His third unhappy adventure harks back ultimately to an ancient Greek fable, related in somewhat different form by Horace,
which tells of a famished fox gorging itself to such an extent on
bread and meat in a hollow tree that it cannot squeeze out through
the opening.[38] Renart leads Primaut to a peasant's cabin where
three hams await them on their entrance through a chink in the
wall. The wolf eats till only his head will fit through the crack
again. The fox pulls him by the ears and by a withe around his
neck, forcing him to yelp and wake the master of the house, who
advances in the dark with a club and a candle. In the first clash
the candle is extinguished. The peasant bends down to relight
it at the fireplace, and the wolf bites his rump, refusing to let
go until the man's wife opens their door to call for help. Primaut
then rips out a hunk of flesh and bolts into the woods, knocking
the woman down. When he finds Renart he tells the fox to taste
the peasant meat, but Renart disdains such unsavory fare. Geese
are preferable, says the fox, and he recommends a gaggle of them
close at hand.

Although the author does not say so, day has presumably
dawned when the wolf invades the flock, only to meet two mastiffs
which Renart has neglected to mention. Able to outrun them,
Primaut furiously mauls the fox for giving bad advice. As he
stomps on Renart's stomach, a whimper for mercy moves him
to pity, and like Ysengrin in *Branche* V he stops short of murdering his counselor.[39] After insisting he knew nothing of the
dogs, Renart threatens to complain at court about the beating
he has suffered, so intimidating Primaut that the wolf proposes
a sacred oath never to harm him again.

Like the fox in Nivardus's perjury episode, Renart takes the
wolf to a place where a saint is supposedly buried but where in
fact a trap is concealed. By kneeling there, the fox declares,
Primaut can make his oath binding. He swears that he will never
hurt Renart again and plops down on the iron teeth, which crush
one foot. Ignoring his pleas for help, the fox skips home to a
warm reception, like the one in *Branche* III.

It is curious that the author does not end XIV at this point but appends another five lines (1084–88), stating no fewer than three times that Renart repents of his wrongdoing. Stressing his contrition through mere reiteration (rather than presenting it elaborately, as in the first 164 lines of *Branche* VIII) is a lame attempt at persuading us to accept what is markedly out of character. The author appears to have felt that we might be scandalized at a sinner who was never sorry, whereas an apology to God would permit Renart to have devil's-food cake, so to speak, and eat it, too. The imp could make heinous mischief without giving offense. Though his remorse is an asinine tail pinned onto the poem, it nevertheless determines how his conduct toward Primaut should be interpreted. It implies that he has persecuted the wolf not because the wolf endangers him, as Ysengrimus menaces Reinardus, but only because he himself is a spiteful prankster, whose behavior is unjustified. The same motive can also be imputed to him vis-à-vis Ysengrin in *Branche* III.

Branche I

In all of the French works so far considered, except the fifteenth *branche,* Renart gets the better of a wolf, like Nivardus's fox. Even V, where he loses a ham to Ysengrin, concludes triumphantly for him, thanks to happenstance. In these poems he is also a threat to little creatures, though the only ones he manages to kill are the hens at the outset of *Branche* IV. In 1620-line I, by contrast, his role becomes more sinister and significant because his prey is all of society. He graduates from being primarily a tormentor of wolves to the status of a subversive at war with the whole establishment, and satire on society again becomes important, as it was in II-Va. There, however, the fox was very much a part of the system being ridiculed—he shared in those faults to which Pierre objected—whereas in *Branche* I he is outside society and the unidentified author's censure of it. In fact, through Renart, who represents him, most of that minstrel's scorn for French leadership at the close of Louis VII's long, inglorious reign (1137–80) is expressed.

In a ten-line prologue he chides Pierre, whom he deprecatingly
calls Perrot, for having forgotten to complete the fox's trial at
King Noble's court. He implies that he will supply a denouement
for Pierre's poem, and *Branche* I is indeed conceived as a continuation of II-Va. Despite the fact that in his prologue the author
of I cites only adultery with Hersent as the charge against Renart,
it—along with Ysengrin's other indictments—is to be superseded
by a more serious complaint.

When the story begins, some ten months must be presumed
to have elapsed since the fox outran Roonel's pack at the end of
II-Va, for the season is spring rather than summer. Ascension
Day (mentioned at the opening of *Branche* XIV) has not yet come.
In a cheerful setting of roses and hawthorn Noble summons the
entire animal kingdom, and only Renart fails to respond, giving
his enemies a splendid chance to blacken him, as in the sick-lion
episode of *Ysengrimus*. Though the wolf is no longer said to be
an official of any kind, he provides a transition from II-Va by out-
shouting everyone else in a call for the vindication of his besmirched honor. He recounts how the fox raped Hersent, urinated
on her cubs, and reneged on the oath of innocence imposed.

Again the monarch winks at illicit love, joking that nowadays
even his own like are cuckolded, as Louis VII was rumored to
have been by Eleanor of Aquitaine. Brun the bear, who is still
Ysengrin's chief supporter, chides Noble for such indifference
and requests a proper hearing, for which he would be willing to
fetch the defendant. Bruyant the bull, a character we did not
meet in II-Va, bellows that the disreputable fox's notorious affair
needs no adjudication and that Ysengrin ought to dispense justice
himself. Grimbert the badger, Renart's cousin, asserts that the
fox's love for Hersent has done no damage and that a trial would
compromise her even more than her husband's accusation. Swearing by the Virgin that she is chaste as a nun, she volunteers to
prove her fidelity in an ordeal (essentially repeating her offer to
Ysengrin after Renart's visit in II-Va). She so convinces Bernart
of her sincerity that he wishes all women were as faithful, but
Bernart is only an ass.

In general Noble's subjects feel that the fox must testify, while their king is more indulgent. So long as loyalty to the crown is maintained, he prefers to overlook a petty squabble between vassals. When the wolf threatens war against Renart, Noble vehemently objects, observing that the fox would probably beat him and reminding him that peace has been officially established throughout the land. It cannot be broken with impunity. The vengeance which Hersent back in II-Va suggested the court might provide is therefore to be conclusively withheld, so that a gloomy Ysengrin slumps to the ground, his tail between his legs. The end of hostilities, alleged to the titmouse in II-Va, has become fact rather than fiction in *Branche* I and is a precondition for Noble's eventual condemnation of Renart.

Scarcely has His Majesty informed us that the truce is in effect when Chantecler, Pinte, and three other hens bring proof that the fox has broken it. On a bier they carry the mutilated corpse of Pinte's sister Copee. To the court Pinte wails that after butchering her five brothers and her four other sisters Renart murdered Copee yesterday and fled before their master, Gonbert del Frenne (rather than Constant des Noes), could catch him. On completing her tale of woes, Pinte faints, together with the other female members of Copee's cortege, and solicitous knights sprinkle their faces with water. When they regain consciousness, they join Chantecler at the feet of the king in pleading for revenge. Noble, who has not been perturbed by Ysengrin's complaints, is furious over the chickens', thundering so loudly and thumping himself so viciously with his tail that everyone quakes. Couart the hare, an important new character in the *Roman de Renart*,[40] comes down with a fever. Because the lion promises Pinte to have the fox punished in her sight, however, Ysengrin is thrilled. The crime against Copee even induces Noble to accept the rape charge now. On behalf of the plaintiffs he accuses Renart of both disturbing the peace and adultery.

Before summoning the fox, he orders a funeral service for Copee. Brun officiates, being a priest in *Branche* I (perhaps as a gibe at sacerdotal corpulence), while Bruyant digs a grave. When the second day of the story dawns, Copee is buried in a leaden casket, with an epitaph proclaiming that she was "martyred" by the fangs of Renart. Noble then dispatches an eager Brun to fetch the fox, and the bear jiggles off on a horse, it seems, because he is said to have one later (line 580).

In this poem, which set a regrettable precedent for subsequent *branches*, various animals appear to be actually mounted at times and not just described as if they were, or instead of merely pretending to be, like Pierre de Saint-Cloud's Tibert.[41] The cat really rides in *Branche* XV, of course, but he crouches atop the saddle and is transported passively to Rufrangier's abode. He is not sufficiently humanized to have feet in the stirrups and hands on the reins, controlling his palfrey.[42] It is also unfortunate that the author of I leaves us unsure whether figures are equestrian or not. His intentions may well have been inconsistent.

The pause in the action caused by Brun's journey is used for a burlesque of miracles, in which Couart is cured of his fever by lying on Copee's grave. Taking advantage of this opportunity to increase opposition to Renart, Ysengrin feigns relief from an earache, on Roonel's recommendation, after likewise reposing above the "martyr's" remains.[43]

When the scene shifts to Malpertuis (consistently a burrow in *Branche* I but often referred to as if it were a castle), we find big Brun, who cannot go in, calling Renart to come outside. The fox justifies his absence by modifying Reinardus's rationalization from the sick-lion episode of *Ysengrimus*. He implies that he has stayed at home because as a pauper he would not be fed well at court. While the rich dine sumptuously there, he pouts, the poor must eat from their lap, fending off dogs which snap at their meager fare.

Even if Renart really is impoverished, he would not be subjected to such indignities, because he is also a baron. His author, as a jongleur, might very well have suffered them, however. The fox's complaint, which is bitterly expressed, reads like a statement of his author's own resentment. If indeed it is, as other critics have thought[44] then a grudge against the privileged helps explain why Renart is cast in the role of a left-wing radical. Through a rebel who snipes at the elite the author could revel in vicarious revenge for being demeaned as a mere entertainer.

The fox seduces Brun by fibbing that he has just enjoyed some honey. With an exclamation in broken Latin, reminiscent of Ysengrin's *nomini dame* in *Branche* III, the bear neglects his duty as emissary, galloping after Renart to the home of a woodsman named Lanfroi. A large split log, held open by wedges, has a honeycomb down inside, says the fox. When Brun sticks his snout and forepaws into the crack, Renart manages to pull the wedges out, clamping him fast. Until Lanfroi appears, the fox makes fun of the bear, scoffing that he wants to keep all the honey to himself. Renart then scoots away, leaving Brun for the fate which the forester prepares by solicting help from a nearby village, like the priest in *Branche* XIV.

Soon peasants—some of whom are satirized by being named as floridly as gentry—swarm through the woods, armed with clubs, hoes, and flails. Lanfroi leads them, brandishing an ax. In order to escape, the bear must yank himself from the log, tearing the hide from his face and paws and leaving both ears behind. Evidently he is not able to mount up at once (if we assume that he does have a horse), for he is dealt many a blow, including one by the local priest, who has been spreading manure and nearly knocks him down with a pitchfork. Eventually Brun escapes, and as he passes Malpertuis Renart jeers at him again, wanting to know which order he belongs to, since he wears a scarlet "hood." We are reminded of Reinardus with the skinned wolf in the sick-lion episode of *Ysengrimus,* but even more similar is the fox mocking the flayed bear in *Aegrum Fama Fuit,* although that bear is the reverse of Brun—having lost hide everywhere except on his head and paws. When Brun reaches court, collapsing from loss of blood, the king bellows oaths and tears out mane in a tantrum. After vowing to avenge the bear, Noble orders the cat to bring Renart, and less for trial than for punishment.

Like the Tibert section of *Branche* XIV, Brun's calamity probably derives from his story in II-Va of how the fox used him as a stalking horse,[45] while the cat's mission now is patterned after the bear's. Tibert will also suffer because desire for a delicacy will

make him incautious, even though he is apprehensive rather than
complacent like Brun when he departs on what is termed his
mule, praying for safety. As if anticipating the future, he addresses his prayers not only to God but also to Saint Leonard,
"who liberates captives."

It is perhaps not for nothing that we are told he starts out
"to the left,"[46] and upon his arrival at Malpertuis in the evening
a "Saint-Martin's bird" flies ominously to his left instead of to
his right. Fearing the worst from Renart, whom he considers an
atheist, Tibert does not venture into the den but halloos in Brun's
manner. Since words cost nothing, as the author remarks, Renart
croons back an amicable welcome and offers to face Noble obediently. Put off guard, the travel-weary cat requests something
to eat. He is promised his fill of mice and conducted to the house
of the priest who hit Brun with a pitchfork. Like his colleague
in *Branche* V, this curé has a problem with rodents, or at least
the fox says he does. At Renart's urging Tibert springs through
a hole in the wall, only to be caught by a snare which the priest's
illegitimate son Martin (heralded by the "Saint-Martin's bird")
laid for the chicken-stealing fox. Renart's designs on the cat,
which failed in both II-Va and XV, finally succeed.

As Tibert is strangled, Martin awakens his parents. The clergyman rises naked from his bed, holding his genitals, while the
concubine lights a candle, wielding her distaff. The scene calls
to mind Primaut's skirmish with the peasant couple in *Branche*
XIV, and just as the wolf bit out a chunk of buttock under
duress, so pummeled Tibert claws out one of his unchaste assailant's testicles. The author of I may also have been influenced
by *Branche* XV, where the cat rends Rufrangier. The suitably
punished lover is incapacitated in I, his mistress swoons, and
Martin tries to revive her, so that Tibert can escape. Since Renart
has disappeared, the cat returns to court alone, bitter at being
so cruelly deceived but partially consoled by thinking that the
amorous priest can henceforth "ring" with only one "clapper."

When, on the third day of the action, Tibert informs the king
of what has happened, Noble does not again fly into a rage but,
feeling rather helpless, simply commands Grimbert to fetch the

renegade. The badger requests an official warrant stamped with a royal seal to certify his authority. Armed with it, he reaches his destination at dusk, after passing through a meadow, a forest, and a clearing, but no mention is made of a valley which both Brun and Tibert traverse. Since Grimbert is Renart's cousin, he is not afraid to enter the den, though he does creep in backwards. He is cordially received and dined at home instead of being led off to a trap in the mere expectation of food.

Only after supper does he broach the reason for his visit. In a funk portrayed by the author as genuine, however much it seems out of character for such a wanton spirit, Renart reads the summons, which threatens him with torture if he fails to be present on the following day to hear his death sentence pronounced. He asks his cousin for advice, and Grimbert recommends that he unburden himself of his sins. In the absence of a priest the badger can serve as father confessor (like the cricket in *Branche* V).

The fox consents, perhaps to amuse himself with a recollection of his fondest capers but surely not to save his soul as he claims. He really did commit adultery with Hersent, he admits, and he hurt Ysengrin in many more direct ways. For example, he says, he caused the wolf to fall into a pit trap and be thrashed after seizing a lamb (reminiscent of the eleventh-century Latin poem *Sacerdos et Lupus*);[47] to be caught again and beaten by three shepherds; to devour hams and be prevented by a bloated belly from escaping (as in *Branche* XIV); to be frozen into the ice while fishing (*Ysengrimus* and *Branche* III); to descend into a well at night, thinking the full moon's reflection was a big cheese (*Branche* IV and *Disciplina Clericalis*); to try deceiving fish merchants (*Branche* XIV); and to become a monk yet profess to be a canon when discovered eating meat (according to a Latin poem, *De Lupo,* from around 1100).[48] Whereas it is Pierre de Saint-Cloud's wolf who sets the plot of *Branche* I in motion, the wolf of Renart's confession is once more Nivardus's, as in *Branches* III, IV, V, and XIV.

The fox acknowledges further that he has sinned not only against Ysengrin but also against every other beast in the king's

court. Specifically he mentions the previous night's hoodwinking
of Tibert, the decimation of Pinte's clan, and (otherwise unknown) a trick he played on an army hired by Ysengrin: after
defeating the wolf's mercenaries, he stole their pay, he concludes
in contrite tones. Admonishing him not to backslide should God
prolong his life, Grimbert absolves him from his sins.

The next morning, early in the fourth and last day of *Branche*
I, Renart kisses his family good-bye and bids his sons to defend
his "castle" by "raising its bridges." Because it is impregnable,
as he says and the end of the poem will confirm, he has no need
either to obey the summons or to be afraid. He even has plenty
of food now, in contrast to his situation in every one of the
previous *branches,* where hunger is his motive for embarking on
adventures. In lines 1121–22 he asserts that Malpertuis is sufficiently stocked to withstand a siege of "seven years." Why,
under these circumstances, does he risk his life at court, except
that the poem's plot depends on his compliance?[49] Be that as it
may, he indulges in more religiosity (comparable to his confession) by praying for acquittal and revenge,[50] by falling prostrate
to pronounce himself three times a sinner, and by warding off
devils with a sign of the cross. Such hypocrisy will later save him
from the gallows.

After crossing a stream, mountains, and a plain, he and the
badger lose their way in a forest and chance upon a prosperous
farm run by nuns. The author states that the travelers err on
account of the fox's grief, yet at the cloister Renart is not too
distraught to allege that the direction they need to take is past
the chicken coop. Grimbert scolds him vigorously for relapsing,
whereupon the fox meekly yields, but as they journey on he
repeatedly turns a wistful gaze toward the nunnery, evidencing
his hopelessly vulpine nature. If his head were cut off, the author
comments, it would fly to that poultry.

We are told that Renart is again afraid of what will befall him
at court and that his horse expresses this fear by stumbling, while
Grimbert's mule trots smoothly along. At their arrival, nevertheless, the tardy delinquent addresses King Noble in a self-
assured manner. With his head held high he asserts that he is

the most valuable of barons and declares that he has been slandered by jealous, egotistic flatterers who would ruin the realm if heeded. Brun and Tibert have only themselves to blame for being caught, he continues, and he has not mistreated Hersent because she and he have been in love. Copee and the other butchered fowl he wisely forbears to mention. He concludes his speech with an appeal for pity, averring that he is too old and weak—the hair on his chest is turning white[51]—to argue with the sovereign, who may dispose of him at will but ought to be fair.

Undeterred by this rhetoric, Noble snarls that Renart will not be spared unless he can clear himself. Grimbert warns that the fox, according to law, must be allowed to refute in public any accusation against him. Instead of granting due process, however, Noble is swayed by Renart's many enemies, who protest the badger's call for a fair trial. Without permitting any defense whatsoever, the arbitrary king requests a sentence from the mob, which clamors for a hanging. Hastily a gallows is erected, for Noble wants the fox strung up before he can escape.

As the crowd torments Renart, Couart casts stones from a safe distance, but a menacing shake of the prisoner's head still sends that poltroon scampering to a hedge, where Renart will later seize him. In *Branche* V the fox excuses himself from Ysengrin with the pretext of a pilgrimage to Santiago Compostella. Here he tells the king that he wishes to atone for his sins by going to the Holy Land. Noble's initial fondness for the colorful cavalier is rekindled, making the king most fickle, though he accedes to Renart's request only on condition that the dangerous adventurer remain permanently in exile. To the dismay of the multitude, Renart is therefore dressed as a pilgrim, pardoned, and released. The author states that the charlatan feels contempt for everyone but the royal couple, yet that observation must be ironic. Renart will soon insult Noble, and he swindles Noble's consort Fere[52] out of a ring by promising to pay for it a hundred times over with prayers in her behalf.

By three in the afternoon he is able to depart, but the author states that he does so on his horse rather than on foot, and instead of heading for Jerusalem he contents himself with the hedge where the hare, a nice dinner for his pups at home, is lurking. When Couart tries to gallop away (for suddenly a mount is credited even to him), Renart grabs his reins (perhaps only metaphorically) and pierces him with the staff that is part of a pilgrim's accoutrement. Dangling the hare from his own saddle, if indeed he has one, Renart appears on the tallest of four rocks that tower above the court. After wiping his rear with his borrowed gear, he hurls it at Noble, shouting that the sultan of Syria and Egypt, Nur-ud-din,[53] sends greetings and that all heathens tremble before the Christian king.

Such is his scorn for the leader of that social system on which he has preyed (a scorn no doubt reflecting the author's attitude toward Louis VII, who was humiliated in the Second Crusade, 1147–49), but the establishment finally gains a modicum of revenge. Renart's indignity and an entreaty from wounded Couart, who is said to free himself from the fox's horse and ride his own to the court, move Noble to order a chase, vainly threatening death to the whole assembly if Renart escapes. An army of knights (led by Tardif the snail!)[54] pursues the obnoxious fox all the way to Malpertuis, "where he fears neither host nor assault," nipping his fur and stabbing his flanks in a climactic scene obviously inspired by the close of Pierre de Saint-Cloud's epic.[55] More like *Branche* XIV, however, I concludes with a vignette of the hero ensconced at home amidst his doting family, although he does not repent of his misdeeds here. Instead, Hermeline, Percehaie, Malebranche, and Rovel, "more beautiful than the others" (perhaps because the author of I created the third son), lavish attention on their master until he recuperates.

Branche I presents a series of outrages perpetrated by the fox against his fellow animals. Ysengrin's grievances against him are taken over from II-Va, and Pinte's also result from wrongs committed before the story begins, while we see his abuse of Brun, Tibert, Couart, and Noble. Those whom he afflicts in this work range from the weakest to the strongest among the nobility and comprise a kind of cross section through that social class which is Renart's actual enemy, even though he belongs to it himself. The poem is unified by the fact that each individual conflict between the fox and another creature (or a family, in Pinte's case) is an aspect of his conflict with the establishment as a whole. Appropriately, all the knights—except Grimbert, of course—take part in the grand pursuit at the end.

Renart is a rogue, as the author repeatedly recognizes,[56] but he is still heroic, like all great villains, while his victims are gullible (Brun and Tibert), effete (Couart and the chickens), cuckolded (Ysengrin), or derelict (Noble), thus becoming contemptible. Because they represent the power structure, it is ultimately that bastion of authority and privilege which is satirized. The author longed to punish the feudal order he knew for its failings and apparently also for its disdain of him, but the court's superiority en masse constitutes an admission that the system was too strong for him, no matter how much he disliked it. What chafed could not be changed. Besides expressing his dissatisfaction with the state, he also wished to make fun of religion and the peasantry (especially as combined in the village curé), probably under the influence of *Branche* XIV.

Along with Pierre's original Reynard poem in French, *Branche* I was favored with unusual popularity, evidenced by the string of half a dozen works which it inspired. They are *Branches* Ia, VI, X, and XXIII, plus the Franco-Italian delight *Rainardo e Lesengrino* and the Flemish masterpiece *Van den Vos Reynaerde*. We will have occasion to deal with *Branche* VI in Chapter Four, but *Van den Vos Reynaerde* is our immediate concern.

Chapter Three
Van den Vos Reynaerde

This most admired and controversial of all the Reynard epics can be accurately interpreted only in comparison with *Branche* I of the *Roman de Renart*. Although developed with a great deal more independence, the second half still reflects some motifs in that French model, and the first half follows *Branche* I rather closely—up to the point at which the fox is about to be hanged.

The fact that the second half is much more original than the first suggests the possibility of double authorship,[1] and in the initial ten lines of the prologue someone who calls himself Willem declares that he was moved to compose the work because an earlier Reynard poem in Dutch was left uncompleted, by a man whom Manuscript F identifies as Arnout. Thus Willem seems to have added in his own way to the free translation which Arnout made of lines 11–1350 from *Branche* I.

As further evidence that more than a single person composed *Van den Vos Reynaerde,* we will notice a number of inconsistencies between the first 1,885 verses (minus the forty-line prologue) and the next 1,444, particularly with regard to King Nobel.[2] Through what we will presume to call Arnout's *Proto-Reinaert* the lion lives up to his name much better than in Willem's continuation, and also better than in *Branche* I. Primarily because of that difference the whole way of life which Nobel represents is treated more positively in *Proto-Reinaert.* Whereas Willem thumbs his nose at a band of dullards trying to impose restrictions on their intellectual superior, Arnout was probably intent on vindicating tradition. There is even good reason to believe that some third, anonymous person added the last 140 lines, with a purpose different from either Arnout's or Willem's. The oft-asserted notion that *Van den Vos Reynaerde* is too unified to have more than one author is erroneous.

We will begin with the actual story, saving the prologue for later analysis, and in the main we will follow Manuscript A, which is all in all the best, taking note of variants when they seem important.[3]

Arnout's *Proto-Reinaert*

As in *Branche* I, the king calls his subjects together in the full bloom of spring, though on Whitsunday rather than near Ascension Day. Everyone responds except the fox. In contrast to the author of *Branche* I, Arnout accounts for the convocation and for the sole conspicuous absence. Nobel holds court to be honored,[4] while Reinaert is afraid of being punished for his crimes, like the fox when *Branche* VI begins. (See Chapter Four.) With respect to Reinaert's guilty conscience, all surviving texts apart from A (these being F, B, and L) allude to John 3:20, which reads, "Everyone who does evil hates the light and shuns it, lest his wrongs be exposed." Either Arnout or an early copyist thereby links the fox to darkness and Nobel to its positive antithesis right at the outset.

Backed by kinsmen, Isengrijn the wolf begs for pity and makes essentially the same speech his counterpart delivers in *Branche* I, for he accuses Reinaert of having degraded both his wife, Hersuint, and their cubs (two of whom were blinded, as we noted in regard to the wolf-den episode of *Ysengrimus*) and of having refused to swear an oath of innocence. Isengrijn presents these charges as merely the worst of a multitude of grievances against his archfoe, however, and Nobel does not disparage him but keeps silent while other animals plead either for or against the fox.

From the wolf's opening denunciation up to the arrival of Cantecleer the cock, Arnout departs from *Branche* I, where in an unstructured manner the question of Hersent's infidelity is debated. For a neater and richer introduction Arnout substituted a double series of two accusers and one defender who rise to lodge or rebut various charges against Reinaert, only the first of which is Isengrijn's imputation of adultery. The second plaintiff is the Frenchified lapdog Cortois, who whines that one winter the fox snitched his only food, a sausage. Thereupon Tibeert the cat speaks up angrily in behalf of Reinaert, explaining that the fox took that sausage many years ago, after Cortois had stolen it from Tibeert, who had pilfered it from a sleeping miller.

Beginning a new set of incriminations, Pancer the beaver relates that, only the day before, he heard Cuwaert the hare learning the Apostles' Creed from Reinaert. Pancer approached for a look just as Cuwaert was seized by the throat. Had the beaver not intervened, the fox would have bitten off his tasty pupil's head, even though Nobel has recently ordered a suspension of all hostility throughout the animal kingdom.

Isengrijn seconds the beaver in demanding that this outrage be punished, but Grimbeert the badger, who is Reinaert's nephew, argues heatedly that the wolf has inflicted more grief on the fox than he has received. For instance, says Grimbeert, Isengrijn gobbled up all the turbot which Reinaert threw down from a cart and consumed a ham which the fox had secured at risk of life and limb (as in both *Ysengrimus* and *Branche* V of the *Roman de Renart,* except that Reinaert was thrown into a·sack). Consonant with *Branche* I, Grimbeert diminishes the fox's guilt vis-à-vis Hersuint by pointing out that the couple have been fond of each other for a long time. If the lady granted her lover's request, no harm was done. As for Cuwaert, the badger queries, is a teacher not empowered to correct his student? Tibeert has already annulled Cortois's accusation, so Grimbeert merely cites the proverb "ill-gotten, ill-fated," which he mispronounces in Latin.

Having more or less parried every thrust at his absent uncle, he closes his defense by asserting that since Nobel proclaimed the ban on feuds Reinaert has been living like a hermit. The penitent has abandoned his "castle"[5] and is even wearing a hair shirt while subsisting on charity and doing penance for his sins. What is more, he has not partaken of meat for a whole year, the badger contends. Grimbeert does not invent this tale, for much of what he says will soon be confirmed, and he states that word of his uncle's vegetarianism was brought the day before by a visitor. He seems to believe sincerely in Reinaert's reform, having not yet heard of the depredations which Cantecleer is about to report.

In *Branche* I Pinte and company cause Noble to change his mind about the fox, while in *Proto-Reinaert* Cantecleer embarrasses Grimbeert by proving that the badger's high opinion of the fox is wrong. As Grimbeert is still pleading his misguided case for Reinaert, the rooster comes into view, descending into the valley where court is convened, and no sooner does Grimbeert finish than Cantecleer arrives. He is followed by two hens, Pinte and Sproete, and by two other cocks, the four of whom are his surviving progeny. Pinte and Sproete carry a bier, on which lie the mangled remains of their dead sister Coppe. The fox beheaded her on the same day that he nearly decapitated Cuwaert.

Cantecleer leaps into the circle of courtiers sitting before the throne, to tell a story different from Pinte's in *Branche* I. After begging for pity with almost the same words used by Isengrijn, he declares that in the joy of early April he had eight sons and seven daughters safe in a beautiful barnyard. Dogs guarded them, keeping Reinaert away, until the fox showed up as a contrite recluse who had pilgrimaged to the Benedictine priory Elmare in Flanders, was wearing the hair shirt mentioned by Grimbeert, and bore a copy of the king's letter instituting peace throughout the land. (Although reminiscent of the birch bark in Nivardus's Sprotinus episode, it was apparently genuine.) Much as Renart in religious guise attempts to beguile the cricket in *Branche* V of the *Roman de Renart,* so Reinaert informed Cantecleer that the poultry need fear him no more, for he was eschewing meat, in accordance with Grimbeert's testimony. He had grown so old, he said, that he had to look out for his soul, and as he went away he read the creed which Cuwaert later wanted to learn from him. When gullible Cantecleer took the brood of fifteen outside their enclosure, trusting the herald of peace, that hypocrite absconded with one of them. Since then he has murdered ten more, the latest victim being Coppe.

Arnout's Nobel, who has remained completely quiet to this point and not compromised himself by protecting the fox like his Gallic compeer, also does not thunder like the latter. Displaying a taciturn reserve and dignity that is a marked improvement over the French king's furor, he merely rasps sarcastically to Grimbeert, "Your uncle the hermit has fasted so well that if I live one more year he'll know it!" A funeral service is performed for Coppe, but Bruun the bear does not officiate, being no priest here, and a night does not intervene.[6] Still on the first day of the action in *Proto-Reinaert* the dead hen is laid to rest under a linden tree. Her casket may not be of lead, but she has a marble tombstone with an epitaph similar to Copee's.

Following the burial in *Branche* I, Noble arbitrarily dispatches Brun, though his barons do urge him to chastise Renart. Here in Arnout's version there are a couple of differences which indicate that in moving from France to Flanders the lion became more democratic as well as more controlled. In accordance with feudal custom he invites consultation, adopting his court's suggestion that the bear should summon the fox. He also shows more concern than the French king, warning Bruun to guard against trickery and disgrace. Instead of even possibly straddling a horse, the oaf lumbers off on foot, indignant at the thought of being shamed.

Arnout included a fair amount of anthropomorphism. Reinaert has been said to wear a cilice, for example, despite all the fur protecting his skin from prickles, but Arnout balked at the incongruity of humanized animals (big as a bear or small as a hare, moreover) riding other beasts which are not humanized. Both Willem and the author of *Reinaerts Historie* maintained his policy in this respect, so that throughout the Dutch and Low-German Reynard epics a creature's only means of transportation is definitely his own legs.

Still another departure from *Branche* I is Arnout's omission of any miracle transpiring on the dead Coppe's grave. Since Nobel does not explode, Cuwaert contracts no fever, but had Arnout wanted to match his mentor in spoofing miracles he could easily have substituted another sickness to be cured. He seems to have been unwilling to mock a belief of the Church.

Without any delay we accompany Bruun across a forbidding landscape of woods (called dark in every text except Manuscript

A), wilderness, and mountains to the mouth of Manpertuus, where he announces that the fox must either render account of himself or be broken on a wheel. Reinaert's response, from the depths of his den,[7] is a modification of Renart's in *Branche* I, for he asserts that he would have come to court voluntarily had he not incurred indigestion from a "strange new food." Renart's rich-man-poor-man speech, which reads like a personal statement by the author of *Branche* I, is expunged by Arnout, who evidently considered it unsuitable. We may thus infer that he harbored no grudge against society. Reinaert tells Bruun only that have-nots must sometimes eat what disagrees with them, so he has made do with honey. The bear begs for some, seductively terming the fox "sweet nephew" and promising to be his friend at court. Relieved at this subservience, Reinaert leads Bruun down a crooked path, figuratively as well as literally.

When the French bear is trapped in *Branche* I, he acts surprisingly subdued, and Lanfroi merely happens by. Arnout's carpenter is brought in likelier fashion by Bruun's agonized shrieks, once the Flemish bear's forepaws and head have been gripped by a giant log. The fox still has enough time for a quick gibe perhaps inspired by Nivardus's surveyor episode, however. Now that Bruun has eaten, Lamfroyt will quench his thirst, Reinaert jests.

To avoid being served, too, the fox scampers off toward home, while the carpenter runs to the village for assistance. Armed with whatever lay at hand, the whole community soon attacks. The local priest wields a crosier, which his sacristan did not want to give him, so that at his first appearance he seems irreligious. During Brun's adventure in *Branche* I the French curé is not lampooned in any extant manuscript and is only briefly mentioned, swinging a pitchfork. The Flemish clergyman's dubious conduct at this point in *Proto-Reinaert* is Arnout's addition, probably prompted by Bovo in the fishing episode of *Ysengrimus*. The sexton charges at Bruun with a flagpole from the church, and Madam Julocke, the cleric's "wife," waves the distaff which her equivalent, omitted from the storming throng in *Branche* I, used against Tibert the cat there. It identifies her as a woman, just as her lover's weapon is also emblematic. Lamfroyt's is, too, being an ax like Lanfroi's, and the fact that the leader of the pack brandishes the most dangerous instrument is quite appropriate. Taking a cue from his French model, Arnout derides these peasants by depicting them as bluebloods.

At the hue and cry Bruun yanks himself free, flaying his head and front feet but losing only one ear instead of two (except in Manuscript B). During the melee which follows, he knocks five harridans, including Julocke, into a nearby river. Because the priest frantically promises absolution from all sins for anyone who dives to the rescue of his floundering bedmate (as Bovo tells parishioners to chase Reinardus if they want to be prayed for), attention shifts from the bear to Julocke, permitting Bruun to plunge into the water himself and swim away. For half a mile he drifts downstream, cursing both the log and Reinaert, before he drags himself ashore.

Major contributions by Arnout are both the priest's abuse of his office in recovering his "wife" from the river and the river's very presence, which enables Bruun to escape not only because the danger of Julocke's drowning diverts the harassers but also because the bear has no horse and can put no weight on his painful forepaws. If Arnout was loath to make fun of miracles, he surpasses his French predecessor in ridiculing the cleric who is unworthy of holy orders, yet his satire on the degenerate pastor is not scorn for the sacred Church. Indeed, it is a defense of the Church insofar as it punishes deviation from her standards.

After abandoning Bruun, Reinaert started for home. Arnout seems to have forgotten momentarily that the bear would not be passing the fox's den, as in *Branche* I. Reinaert has to meet his victim by the river. On a lonely mountaintop he has consumed a hen, much like his counterpart in the fishing episode of *Ysengrimus*. Since the burning sun has parched his throat, he prances down to the water, smug over the presumed slaughter of Bruun. In *Branche* I the fox does not intend for the bear to die, but he definitely does in *Proto-Reinaert*. In lines 900–905 we are explicitly told that he hopes Lamfroyt has beaten Bruun to death, the bear being the greatest threat to him at court. As the largest of the animals Bruun might be most able to injure the petite fox, but he has no reason to and has even pledged his support. Reinaert's hollow rationalization does not begin to justify the enormity wrought against an innocent dupe. We see that Arnout's fox will kill on the slightest pretext. His discovery of Bruun infuriates him. Elaborating on Renart's question in *Branche* I about which order the bloody bear belongs to, because of his red "hood," Reinaert refers to a "tonsure" which includes one ear and to "gloves" left behind. Perhaps evening prayers are to be chanted, flouts the fox, now that the first day of the plot is drawing to a close.[8] Unlike Renart, Reinaert also vaunts his wickedness, speaking proudly of himself as a cruel scoundrel.

The reason why Bruun is not a real priest, in contradistinction to the French bear, may be that Arnout did not want an acceptable cleric mishandled as Bruun has been. Lamfroyt's pastor, who will be mangled in the Tibeert episode, is seriously remiss, whereas Bruun's worst fault is a passion for honey. That Arnout sympathized with the bear is indicated by the word "poor" (*arm*) which he uses in regard to Bruun during the latter's ordeal—lines 773, 838, and 934.[9] The way in which he presents Bruun contributes to our emerging image of Arnout as someone who sided with Church and state, law and order, rather than with rebels like the fox.

At Reinaert's jeers the aching bear feels that his heart will break. Since he is incapable of taking revenge, he hurls himself back into the river and drifts downstream far enough to escape his persecutor. The river will not carry him the extra mile to court, and neither will his hideless front feet. For a while he shoves himself backwards on his bottom, but he makes faster progress by rolling, like bloated Ysengrimus early in Nivardus's pilgrimage episode.

Saddened that his deputy has been mistreated, Nobel swears to retaliate. Despite his ire, however, he is again much more composed than the lion in *Branche* I, for instead of tearing his mane with a roar and impulsively dispatching Tibeert without consultation, he calmly parleys with his barons, who advise a second summons, delivered by the small but sagacious cat. Reinaert trusts Tibeert, some of the counselors believe, but Tibeert is still reluctant to undertake such a dangerous mission. Even though Nobel encourages him with more considerateness than the French king shows, he sets out just as timorously as *Branche* I's cat.

He does not depart to the left, but the "Saint-Martin's bird" which flies to the left appears in the course of his journey. Tibeert presses on, finding a confident fox outside Manpertuus, as if expecting him, in all texts but A. Immediately after bidding Reinaert a good evening, for the sun has indeed set, the cat relays his message. The fox ignores it and welcomes Tibeert as his "nephew," moving Arnout to comment parenthetically, "What does pretty talk cost Reinaert?" In inserting this remark, Arnout imitates his French predecessor, but he adds that the fox's friendly tongue belies a wicked heart.

Reinaert invites his adoptive kinsman to spend the night at Manpertuus, agreeing to heed the summons at daybreak. Though the moon shines brightly, as impatient Tibeert points out, the fox asserts that traveling by night is too dangerous. The Flemish cat is warier of his host than the hungry French cat is, but he eventually yields to Reinaert's determined hospitality, provided the food is good. Teasing Tibeert, the fox replies that he does not have much of a menu but that he can offer some delicious honey. Thus he reverses the pose assumed with Bruun. When Tibeert asks instead for mice, Reinaert avers that a priest in the area has a barn overrun by them.

With no more ado the fox escorts the cat to the granary from which he stole a rooster the previous day (or night, according to texts other than A) and where he coaxes Tibeert into a snare set by the curé's son Martinet. Before being caught, the cat expresses a fear of priests' deception. His low opinion of the clergy is a touch added by Arnout (though derived from lines 848–50 of *Branche* I) and therefore presumably a statement of the author's own sentiments. Arnout was unhappy with many men of the cloth.

Tibeert's screeching awakens Martinet, who rouses his parents and siblings. The pastor no longer holds his genitals, but the number of children has been increased to intimate how active his genitals have been. In *Branche* I we are not told with what he arms himself, only that his mistress grabs her distaff and lights a candle. In *Proto-Reinaert,* however, he takes the distaff and she keeps the candle in what Gerard-H. Arendt calls an "exchange of symbols" which "reveals the curate as a slave to sex" (*als sinnlichen Weiberknecht*).[10] Arendt might have observed as well that both symbols are phallic and that the candle is an *offer keersse,* intended for funeral services.

Three times in eighteen lines our attention is directed to the clergyman's nakedness, whereas *Branche* I's author never overtly mentions it. Clearly Arnout did not want his listeners to be unaware of that profane exposure, which not only underscores the priest's unchasteness but is also a precondition of the maiming perpetrated by Tibeert. After Martinet has knocked out one of the cat's eyes with a stone, his father rears back to deliver the coup de grâce but instead gives up a testicle, as in the source. Arnout's Julocke, who is both less hysterical and more articulate than the French concubine, swears by the soul of her sire that she would rather forgo their income for a year than be so shamed and deprived. "If he recovers from his wounds, he'll flag in the sweet sport," she moans to Martinet.

Renart leaves Tibert with no taunts at all, but in *Proto-Reinaert* the more sadistic fox lingers to twit both the cat and Julocke. He consoles her with the assurance, borrowed from *Branche* I, that it is no disgrace for her amorous athlete to "ring" with one "clapper." He departs for home as the suitably punished lecher swoons. In the French version it is the woman who faints, but the dispossessed owner of that organ on the floor is likelier to do so. Julocke manages to lift her bloodied Adonis and lug him back to bed, permitting the cat to gnaw free. Just as the "wife's" plight saved Bruun, so the "husband's" saves Tibeert.

When the second emissary limps up to Nobel's throne, the second day of the revised story has dawned. Arnout expresses the same sympathy he felt for Bruun, speaking of Reinaert's latest victim also as "poor" (line 1320). The king is outraged to learn of Tibeert's missing eye, which makes the cat more pitiable and

the fox more culpable than their respective counterparts in *Branche*
I, where such a sacrifice is not exacted from Tibert. Again Nobel
collects his barons for advice, instead of simply packing Grimbeert
off with sovereign disregard for his vassals. The badger reminds
the group that by law Reinaert as a free man deserves a third
subpoena. If he then does not respond, he will automatically be
deemed guilty on every count against him. "Whom do you want
to fetch him, Grimbeert," asks the king, for who would risk
personal harm? Nobel has his subjects' welfare too much in mind
to imitate his arbitrary French equivalent, but the badger volunteers as the third envoy. He is so self-assured that he does not
even request a writ. As with Bruun the previous day, the lion
warns him to be careful.

While the bear crossed an eery landscape and the cat met with
an unfavorable omen on the way to Manpertuus, Grimbeert's trip
is in no wise inauspicious. Not a single detail of it is mentioned,
so insignificant is it. Upon his arrival, the badger does not back
timidly into the den or allow his harsh message to be softened
by conviviality. Relying on his kinship and knowing that Reinaert
must obey the third summons, he marches in and politely announces that this is his uncle's final chance to be saved. Manpertuus will be laid open and Reinaert ingloriously executed with
his entire family if he remains recalcitrant, Grimbeert declares,
though by going to court the fox might well be pardoned. On
this last point Reinaert voices doubt, but he acquiesces, since he
has no good alternative. Unlike Malpertuis, his den is indeed
destructible, in accordance with the badger's warning. Neither
dinner nor night has intervened when he bids his wife Hermeline
and their two sons farewell, praising the elder whelp, Reinaerdijn.
His warm relationship with his family is Reinaert's one endearing
trait, yet that is vitiated by his adultery with Hersuint.

Renart's unchristian prayer and mummery on leaving home
is omitted in *Proto-Reinaert,* and the pendant to his confession
during the night in *Branche* I is conducted on the road, since
Reinaert and Grimbeert are not tarrying at Manpertuus. Both
the rationale and the content of the confession are altered, moreover. While even in the French it smacks of braggadocio, the

badger elicits it to assuage the fear which the author says the summons struck into his cousin's heart. In the Flemish, Reinaert himself requests to be shriven, his probable motive being to while away travel time by reliving past triumphs, even though he (but not Arnout) claims that he is anxious. He draws his reminiscences out to more than 200 lines, whereas Renart's last only sixty-seven or so.

Reinaert begins with a cynical parody of sincere confession, for he adds the word *mater* ("Mother") to the standard formula *confiteor pater* ("I confess, Father") and rhymes it with *cater* ("tomcat"). Cursorily he acknowledges having had Bruun scalped and Tibeert bastinadoed. After also admitting that Cantecleer accused him correctly, he alludes to a mysterious disgrace he dealt the king and queen. Possibly he seduced the lioness, though he does not say so, the incident is not otherwise mentioned, and nothing corresponds in the French confession. In *Branche* Ia of the *Roman de Renart,* a continuation of *Branche* I, the fox rapes the queen, [11] and Arnout may have had that knavery in mind.

The rest of the confession—by far the larger part—is a narrative of six crimes against Isengrijn. The first seems to combine influence from the monastery episode of *Ysengrimus* with *Branche* XII of the *Roman de Renart,* where the fox ties Tibert by his neck and feet to a bell rope and the cat, who is thought to be a devil, is thrashed. [12] Reinaert persuaded Isengrijn to become a monk at Elmare, where he bound the wolf's feet to a bell rope after Isengrijn had drunk too much wine. The mad tolling that resulted caused the wolf, who was mistaken for Satan, to be beaten within an inch of his life. Apparently this incident occurred before the visit to Elmare reported by Cantecleer. On a later occasion (suggested by *Branche* III) Reinaert tonsured Isengrijn by burning his scalp. The fishing expedition from *Branche* III and *Ysengrimus,* cited in the *Branche*-I confession, is also touched on here (and greatly expanded in Text L, or *Reynardus Vulpes,* a thirteenth-century translation of *Van den Vos Reynaerde* into 925 Latin distichs).

From *Branche* XIV comes another anecdote referred to in the *Branche*-I confession, but Arnout devotes nearly a hundred lines to it, giving his own version. Reinaert took the wolf to the store house of a rich priest. Through a small opening the fox had Isengrijn crawl inside, to stuff himself on meat. The wolf swelled so much that in trying to exit he became stuck. Reinaert ran into the village, where the pastor sat gobbling in Isengrijn's manner. The fox grabbed a pet capon from in front of the table, leading its furious owner to the store house and dropping it there, as Reinardus lures an angry crowd to the icebound Ysengrimus by stealing Bovo's rooster. After Isengrijn had been discovered and drubbed by a gathering mob, he was tortured by the village children.

Though the gourmandizing churchman, who replaces the peasant of *Branche* XIV, may have been suggested by Arnout's copy of *Branche* I, for three surviving *Roman-de-Renart* manuscripts call the curate's French counterpart a *prevoire,* [13] Arnout wanted at any rate to inject more satire on profane clergy. Not only is the opulent pastor enamored of food; he shouts incorrect Latin in Manuscript A (*sancta spiritus* rather than *sanctus spiritus,* as in line 1534 of Manuscript F), and he conducts himself in a most unseemly fashion—cursing, overthrowing the table, and chasing Reinaert with a carving knife. By adding that crude glutton to Julocke's lover, Arnout broadened his attack on priests whose concerns were more physical than spiritual, yet because those two reprobates are real men, not members of the animal kingdom, Arnout could ridicule carnal clerics without impugning the social order, which is represented by Nobel's court. (In the same way, of course, he was also able to separate peasants—a contempt for whom he clearly shared with Nivardus and the author of *Branche* I—from respectable society. Differing markedly, Willem included no human beings whatsoever in his continuation of *Proto-Reinaert.*)

The fifth practical joke which the fox played on Isengrijn may also have been inspired by the episode in *Branche* XIV about Primaut trapped in the farm house, but it resembles Tibeert's contretemps, as well. In this prank Reinaert offered to provide all the chicken Isengrijn could eat in exchange for a year of service. He took the wolf to a dwelling, in the loft of which twelve hens and a cock were supposedly roosting. Insengrijn climbed in, to grope about in the dark and eventually to tumble down on the sleepers below. Again he was sorely belabored.

The sixth and last sin against him Reinaert claims to regret most of all, but the fox is thinking of adultery, the first matter broached in *Branche* I's confession. He prefers to state obliquely that he "betrayed" Hersuint and that he did something to her which he would rather have left undone. When the badger prods him to be more open, he queries, "Would it be refined of me to say right out that I'd slept with my aunt?" Grimbeert pursues the issue no further, having demanded frankness not because he is nosey but only because he is simple.

In both *Branche* I and *Proto-Reinaert* the confession further documents the fox's disdain for fellow creatures and especially for the wolf. Also, by being traditionally his principal victim, the wolf deserves more attention than the initial accusation at court provides. Arnout accords the wolf greater prominence than does the author of *Branche* I, but Reinaert's confession is all in all less important than Renart's. By first revealing the French fox as a tartuffe, the *Branche*-I confession begins to prepare us for his crucial pose of piety after he is condemned. That function is completely missing from *Proto-Reinaert,* where the fox's false devoutness is introduced much earlier and where it has no bearing on the outcome, as we are soon to see.

Poor Grimbeert thinks his uncle's soul is being saved and deals him forty strokes with a switch as penance, admonishing him to substitute the practices of a true believer for his old rapaciousness. Reinaert professes to be willing, but he quickly goes astray, in a double sense, for he departs from the direct route to court in order to pass a Benedictine convent where geese and chickens feed outside their coop. In *Branche* I Renart and Grimbert happen by a cloister with tempting poultry, having accidentally erred. The fact that in *Proto-Reinaert* the fox intentionally guides his nephew to a nunnery, where he tries to grab a rooster, makes him more cynical than in the source. In both works his disregard for the property of a religious community implies indifference toward religion per se.

The artless badger is so scandalized that Reinaert apologizes, but he glances back at his favorite game. "He couldn't control himself; he had to obey his nature," Arnout interjects, stressing the fox's incorrigibility. From *Branche* I Arnout took the idea that if Reinaert's head were cut off it would fly to those fowls.

As the fox and his nephew approach their destination, Reinaert quakes with fear. While this is the only time in Arnout's poem that the fox shows genuine apprehension, even one moment of doubt before his fate is decided can be difficult to accept. The significance of this moment seems to lie, however, in its anticipation of what is actually to befall him at the end of *Proto-Reinaert*. Of the three fits of anxiety in *Branche* I (when Renart reads the warrant, when he strays en route, and when he draws near to court) Arnout may have kept the last precisely because it suits his conclusion, regardless of psychology.

Upon Reinaert's arrival, all his opponents rehearse their complaints, but like his counterpart in *Branche* I (and also *Branche* VI) he acts undaunted. As if he were Nobel's son and had done nothing wrong, Arnout tells us, he marches to the throne and delivers almost the same speech given by Renart in the source. Rival courtiers would like to deprive him of royal favor, which he has earned by being the crown's most loyal subject, Reinaert claims, but King Nobel will surely not heed them! Too many slanderers have already gained control of governments, injuring good people, he preaches. May God punish them!

Whereas in *Branche* I the lion holds his tongue until Renart has finished speaking, Arnout has him interrupt at this point to set the record straight. According to Manuscripts F and B, which are preferable here to A (lines 1802–1805), Nobel acknowledges Reinaert's services but sneers sarcastically, "You've done a fine job of keeping the peace I established!" After a wail from Cantecleer, who is reminded of Coppe by those words, the lion quips that the fox's vaunted devotion has been demonstrated in his treatment of Bruun and Tibeert. Rebuke is pointless, however, for a hanging appears inevitable, Nobel decides.

With an interjection in flawed Latin,[14] Reinaert disclaims responsibility for the misfortunes of the bear and the cat, like

Renart before him, except that he lies in alleging that he did not advise Tibeert "to go stealing." Though Renart also excuses having made love to Hersent, Reinaert can overlook the wolves because adultery is not an issue at his trial. For the conclusion of his speech he echoes essentially what Renart said about being at the king's mercy, so that punishing him would amount to a bully's meanness. He differs from Renart in omitting any mention of old age, however, which Arnout may have felt would be inconsistent with his lawless behavior and his young family. Reinaert's claim to Cantecleer that he was advanced in years was apparently part of his hoax.

His plea fails, for a host of animals, led by the ram Belijn and by Belijn's mate Hawi, demand a full trial, which the king is also disposed to conduct. In *Branche* I, by contrast, the kangaroo court denies due process. [15] While Arnout paid more heed to justice, he nevertheless ignored details. He would have had to create them completely, and he was too impatient to do so, having reached the end of his poem. All he reports is that exchanges between Reinaert and the other beasts were "beautiful" and that accusations were duly confirmed. Like the French lion (except in Manuscripts B and H of the *Roman de Renart*), Nobel asks his barons how to sentence the defendant, but only after guilt has been determined. As in *Branche* I, hanging is decreed, and Arnout writes in line 1885, "Now it's all up with Reinaert." That the next verses must come from Willem's pen we will see in the section to follow.

At the beginning of this chapter mention was made of Willem's introductory hint that he completed an earlier Reynard poem in Dutch left fragmentary by Arnout. If *Proto-Reinaert* did end at our present line 1885, it could easily have been thought a mere torso by anyone who knew *Branche* I, but at the same time the execution of the renegade implied by a stop at line 1885 would suitably terminate a story undertaken in behalf of the ruling class and standard values. Arnout probably felt that undiscriminating listeners would protest an explicit hanging of the fox, while people perceptive enough to discern his slant would not need a fuller finish. In the part of the prologue he is likely to have composed, as we will see, he declares that he is aiming his words at just such folk—those who are refined.

Because he maintained a basic attitude of dispassionate objectivity, Arnout's subtle bias becomes most evident when his work is compared with its model. For each substantial change he introduced he had to have a reason. Why did he consistently make his head of state a calmer, more democratic, and fairer sovereign than the lion in *Branche* I if he did not want us to view that state positively rather than negatively? At no point in *Proto-Reinaert* is Nobel remiss, and he is never open to ridicule, whereas the French king condones adultery, throws temper tantrums, acts autocratically, and fails to conduct a just trial (to list only those faults of his which occur in the first 1,350 lines of *Branche* I). Like the state, moreover, the Church per se is never demeaned by Arnout, yet his Gallic counterpart mocks the orthodox belief in miracles. Arnout's intensified satire on unfit clergy implies respect, not disrespect, for the sacred side of life, and that respect seems to be confirmed by his refusal to have "poor" Bruun ordained. Finally, his fox is even more brutal than the protagonist of *Branche* I. Arnout must have wanted us to identify with his lawmaker instead of his lawbreaker. That Willem turned those intentions around, we will proceed to ascertain.

Willem's Continuation of *Proto-Reinaert*

Van den Vos Reynaerde starts to diverge conclusively from *Branche* I in line 1886, where Grimbeert and the fox's other kinsmen quit the court in protest over the death sentence, unable to bear the sight of their relative hanged like a thief. The nephew who has played a significant role in *Proto-Reinaert* is thus denied participation in Willem's sequel, but his departure, which does not occur in *Branche* I, will prove to be a prerequisite for Reinaert's crucial speech some 170 lines later. Since that highly original declamation is definitely from Willem's pen, its early preparation must also be Willem's doing rather than Arnout's.

King Nobel is so perturbed by the exodus of Grimbeert and the other dissenters that he silently questions his condemnation of the fox (line 1900). Contradictorily, however, he urges Bruun and Isengrijn to speed up the execution. Night is falling, he observes, and Reinaert might escape. In lines 1346–50 of *Branche* I the lion likewise calls for fast action, lest Renart elude the gallows. Willem seems to have started his continuation uncertainly. After striking out on his own, he sought a moment's support from Arnout's old crutch before resuming his independence. Balduinus, the Latin translator of *Van den Vos Reynaerde,* tried to resolve the resulting illogicality by having the king think that the hanging should be hurried precisely on account of the fox's kin, as if they might otherwise interfere. The author of Manuscript B, which is *Reinaerts Historie,* dealt with the problem better by having Tibeert, not Nobel, tell the bear and the wolf to be quick before the fox slips away.

Another fault committed by Willem as he began to grapple with his story is his carelessness in arranging Reinaert's execution. Far from telling us why the wolf and the bear should do a hangman's dirty work, [16] Willem does not even have Nobel formally assign them the job. As we just saw, the lion (or Tibeert in Manuscript B) merely scolds them for being slow. Willem's reason for having Bruun and Isengrijn ready the gallows is that they, together with the cat, must be removed from the scene like Grimbeert as a preliminary to Reinaert's oration, and the gibbet is some distance from where the court is convened.

Willem was more clever with Tibeert than with the bear and the wolf, though still not clever enough. After the cat has also prodded Isengrijn, reminding him that Reinaert once arranged to have his two brothers hanged, the wolf wonders where a rope can be found. The fox, who claims to want his anguish shortened, points out that the cord from Martinet's snare still dangles from Tibeert's neck. Isengrijn swears by his tonsure that Reinaert's remark is good, and Nobel commands the cat to assist the bear and the wolf, at least in Manuscript A. (In other texts it is the fox who gives that order.) Since Reinaert hankers after cloister beer, jokes Isengrijn, they will brew him some. Willem reminds us of the wolf's career as a monk by alluding to it twice (i.e, through cloister beer and tonsure) because, as we will later be told, it led to the fox's excommunication and that ban will help

save Reinaert. After instructing everyone, but especially his wife
Hersuint, to guard the fox closely, Isengrijn bounds away with
Bruun and Tibeert, spurred on by Reinaert, who still pretends
to yearn for death's release.

It is amazing how quickly the bear's forepaws have healed! He
was forced to roll into court only the day before because he could
put no pressure on those bloody feet, and now Willem has him
gallop forth, jumping obstacles in steeplechase fashion, just as
if Lamfroyt's log were in a different tale. Other evidence of new
authorship at this point is the reference to Isengrijn's brothers,
whose hanging should have been included in the confession to
Grimbeert. Arnout seems not to have known of that event, just
as he also fails to mention Martinet's rope when Tibeert returns
to court. He assumed that all of the snare was left behind, for,
on first seeing the cat again, Nobel notices only that one eye is
missing (lines 1324–25). A rope trailing from Tibeert's neck
would be equally noteworthy. If the cat did drag one all the way
back, moreover (and his counterpart Diebreht does in line 1734
of *Reinhart Fuchs*), he would surely not continue wearing it. It
is not only uncomfortable but also a reminder of his nightmare.
A final point is that Arnout never acknowledges the presence of
Hersuint at court.

Watching Bruun, Isengrijn, and Tibeert disappear, the fox
mutters that he can proceed to trick the king with a ruse he
worked out anxiously during the night. That remark also conflicts
with *Proto-Reinaert*. On the previous night the fox conducted
Tibeert to the priest's barn, where he laughed at the cat and
Julocke. He went home early enough to hatch out a scheme before
dawn, but he can hardly have been care ridden, as Willem has
him profess to have been (line 2045). If he had already devised
a plan for saving himself, moreover, would he have trembled
with fear, as Arnout says he did, when approaching the court?
Arnout gives not the slightest hint that Reinaert had considered
any means of escape other than the speech he delivered upon his
arrival. Perhaps Willem had *Proto-Reinaert* less clearly in mind
than *Branche* I, where Renart is indeed frightened on the evening
before he goes to court, for that is when Grimbert brings the

summons. (In *Reinaerts Historie* the fox has not contrived a stratagem in advance and must concoct one on the spur of the
moment.)

Reinaert's ploy for saving himself is to convince the king that
he has a hoard stashed away (even though he does not), to be
exchanged for his life, as in *Branche* Ia of the *Roman de Renart*
Hermeline ransoms her husband with real gold and silver.[17] Reinaert wants to broach the subject of a treasure as part of a general
confession, in which he would seem to be telling nothing but
the truth, so he requests permission to reveal his many sins,[18]
alleging as his reason the possibility that someone else could be
blamed for what he has done. Since the execution cannot be held
yet anyway and a refusal would be outrageous, Nobel consents.

From the innocence of infancy he graduated to crime when he
killed a lamb who was his playmate, the fox contritely admits.
He liked the taste of blood so much that he quickly became a
wholesale butcher. Eventually, he says, he fell in with Isengrijn,[19]
whom he befittingly met in the dead of winter. The wolf figured
that they were uncle and nephew, even though Reinaert states
in the confession to Grimbeert (lines 1481–82) that he has just
pretended to be Isengrijn's nephew.[20] Because he loved his dear
uncle, the fox continues, he endured the latter's selfishness despite
having acquired a huge amount of wealth.

At mention of riches Nobel pricks up his ears, curious to learn
how Reinaert obtained them. "Sire, that treasure was stolen; but
otherwise you would have been assassinated," the fox announces.
On hearing of a threat against her husband's life, Gente the queen
becomes distraught. In *Proto-Reinaert* her presence at court, like
Hersuint's, is never mentioned. Arnout did not mean for her to
attend the fox's trial, because Fere does not appear in *Branche* I
until after Renart has been pardoned. (See note 52 to Chapter
Two.) Like the French fox, Reinaert greets only the king when
he arrives. Willem nevertheless implies that Gente has been at
Nobel's side all along, and he gives her a vital role in his continuation. Easily excitable as she is, she will serve to reinforce
the fox's artifice, helping to persuade her less impetuous mate.
Whereas Nobel is merely saddened by the news about a murder

plot, his consort enjoins Reinaert to expose that conspiracy, since the fox will soon face heaven or hell. Reinaert therefore launches into an incrimination of his enemies Bruun, Isengrijn, and Tibeert. To lend more credence to his fabrication, he also includes both Grimbeert and his own deceased father. With none of the five present he runs no risk of contradiction, particularly since the king commands everyone to remain silent until he has finished.

He begins his make-believe by affirming that his father discovered an ancient treasure, once upon a time. Because of it the older fox grew arrogant, supposedly, and turned against his former friends, sending Tibeert to Bruun in the Ardennes with an invitation to supplant the lion as king. Apparently Reinaert's father was to be merely the power behind the throne because a fox is not imposing enough to wear a diadem, whereas Nobel might readily believe that the powerful bear is a rival. Bruun accepted the offer, the court is told, and one befittingly gloomy night he, the cat, the wolf, the badger, and Reinaert Senior met in a desolate area near Ghent to pledge the death of Nobel.

Early one morning, the fox continues, a tipsy Grimbeert let Hermeline know what was afoot,[21] and she informed her husband, whose heart, he assures his listeners, was chilled with fear for the commonweal. He was reminded of the fable about ungoverned frogs who prayed for a king, only to be subjected to a ravaging stork.[22] Nobel's kindness would have given way to tyranny, Reinaert maintains, flattering his master shamelessly, for we will see that in fact he fumes over the lion's control. He attempts to embarrass the whole court by adding that for saving his country he has been ill rewarded.

In order to spoil the conspirators' machinations (a role comparable to Elegast's in the Dutch epic *Karel ende Elegast*),[23] he had to find their wherewithal, so he trailed his father, he asserts, until one day he saw the traitor emerge from a hole. In it was the hoard, says Reinaert, which he and Hermeline transferred to another cave while his father was off recruiting a mercenary army. When the elder fox discovered the theft upon his return, he hanged himself in despair, so the story goes, and lack of funds forced the intriguers to abandon their plans for a coup.[24] Nobel's foes are honored, with his benefactor in disgrace, the fox concludes. By alleging that someone else—especially someone now dead—initially unearthed the treasure, he makes its existence more credible than if he purported to have found it first himself, and what reason for having stolen it could appeal to the king more than thwarting sedition?

Seduced by the combination of loyalty and bullion, Nobel and Gente take Reinaert aside, where the rest of the court cannot hear, to ask him bluntly for his fortune. He replies with equal frankness that he would be crazy to let them have it since they are about to hang him. Thereupon the impulsive queen offers him the deal he has expected—his life for a chimera. The king objects that Reinaert is not to be trusted, but Gente insists that he has changed. If he were dishonest, she observes, he would not have sullied his own father and his nephew. Encouraged by the lioness's confidence, Nobel yields to the avarice instilled in him by Willem and forgives the fox, though warning against further mischief.

Thus he repeats the mistake of virtually all Reinaert's victims, for he is swindled in the expectation of gain, yet his greed is more reprehensible. He hopes to fill his purse instead of his paunch and is willing to sacrifice justice, annulling that verdict of his barons which Arnout had him honor. As a token of amnesty he gives the fox a straw in a gesture known as *festucatio*.[25] Reinaert expresses his thanks and symbolically transfers the treasure by handing Nobel another straw. Because the treasure is not worth even a straw, he can hardly suppress his mirth. The head of state who in Arnout's poem was a paragon of respectability has become a contemptible laughingstock in Willem's continuation.

As a location for his fancied lucre Reinaert picks a desolate region of northeast Flanders named Hulsterloo. There, he says, by a spring known to its rare visitors as Kriekeput,[26] Nobel will find the hoard if a little moss is scraped from under the nearest birch. The king dramatically threatens Reinaert's success by raising two objections, however. He wants the fox to accompany him, and he has never heard of Kriekeput, the existence of which

he doubts. Reinaert deals with the second difficulty first, by
calling Cuwaert the hare to come over and testify. Like Nivardus's
Gutero, Cuwaert is easily intimidated, approaching as he does
all aquiver with fright, but he really knows about the spring.
Without having heard what Reinaert has said to Nobel, the hare
affirms that Kriekeput is in the wilderness of Hulsterloo. He is
familiar with it, he adds, because he lived there miserably among
counterfeiters once, before becoming friends with a dog named
Rijn. The fox wishes Rijn were present, to testify poetically how
faithful he has been to the king. [27]

Having dispelled Nobel's suspiciousness, Reinaert sends Cuwaert back to the other courtiers and apologizes that he himself
will not be able to serve as a guide to Kriekeput, being excommunicate. Three years ago a dean named Herman banned him,
he explains, for advising Isengrijn to forswear monasticism, which
was too austere for the wolf. A king should not associate with
someone who has been anathematized, the fox points out, and
Nobel agrees. Just as Renart offers to pilgrimage in *Branche* I,
so Reinaert vows to seek absolution in Rome and head for the
Holy Land.

The reversal for which the fox has been working ever since
Willem's continuation began is finalized when Nobel mounts a
podium of stones and tells his subjects, seated on the grass, that
he and Reinaert have been reconciled. The queen has interceded
for the fox, who wants to reform, he announces, and he warns
that Reinaert must be treated with respect.

Tiecelijn the raven flies to the gallows with word for the three
brewers of cloister beer that the fox has become chief cupbearer,
as he says. Isengrijn and Bruun race back to the assemblage,
while Tibeert, afraid to risk another confrontation with the
hellhound who has already cost him an eye, stays safely on the
gibbet, to which he has attached the cord that nearly strangled
him.

The wolf and the bear prove that the cat's caution is wise, for
Nobel has them bound at once and Reinaert has them maimed,
when they burst upon the court. In *Branche* X of the *Roman de
Renart,* a cross between *Branche* I and the sick-lion episode of

Ysengrimus, the fox has the wolf and Brichemer the stag mutilated
on the pretext of curing the king. If Tibert did not escape through
a window, he would also suffer.[28] In *Van den Vos Reynaerde* a
square foot of hide for a pilgrim's satchel is exacted from Bruun,
while Isengrijn and Hersuint must each donate the skin from two
feet as shoes.

Even before dawn on the third and final day the fox ties on
his shaggy new boots and petitions the king to leave. Nobel
accordingly summons Belijn the ram, whom Willem promoted
to court chaplain. Back in *Proto-Reinaert,* Belijn, who was the
first to protest the fox's attempt at self-exculpation, had a wife,
Hawi (lines 1847–49). Manuscript F refers to her as merely
"someone who came with him," but in Texts A, B, and L she
is definitely his mate. Because of her and the fact that Arnout
did not speak of Belijn as a clergyman, while Willem never
indicates that the ram is still married, we seem to have another
inconsistency resulting from double authorship. Willem's idea
of making Belijn court chaplain probably came from *Branche* VI
of the *Roman de Renart.*[29]

Nobel wants the ram to send Reinaert off with proper ritual,
but Belijn balks on account of the ban. Despite having respected
religious authority enough to shy from going to Kriekeput with
an excommunicate, the king insists on granting that excommunicate an honorable farewell, though the former involvement
would have been his own, whereas the latter is Belijn's. His
observation that according to some theologian (called respectively
Jufroet, Gelijs, and Gelis by Manuscripts A, F, and B) contrite
travelers to the Holy Land can be restored to grace without
ecclesiastic agency[30] does not impress the chaplain, who is thinking only of his bishop's wrath. The lion's wrath becomes more
fearsome, however, since Nobel threatens a hanging for disobe-
dience. Inadequate regard for the Church's demands is another
fault imputable to Willem's king.

Shedding tears of feigned repentance and yet of genuine sorrow,
too, that he could torture only Bruun and the wolves, the fox
begs everyone to pray for him. The king would detain him longer,
but Reinaert is understandably eager to be gone. In his honor,

though also to his chagrin, Nobel enjoins the whole court, except
for the two prisoners, to accompany him partway. The sight of
Public Enemy Number One parading as a man of God would
stir anybody to laughter, Willem chuckles, revealing a fondness
for the fox which Arnout never shows. Like Arnout, who expresses
a low opinion of Reinaert on six different occasions, always terming him cruel *(fel),* [31] Willem speaks negatively of him four times,
acknowledging his ruthless malice. [32] To Willem he was as evil
as he seemed to Arnout, but Willem obviously admired that
devilishness, just as Arnout's fox admires it in himself. Willem's
attitude toward Reinaert resembles that of the author toward
Renart in *Branche* I.

After proceeding a short distance, the pilgrim turns back his
entourage by warning Nobel that Bruun and Isengrijn, as dangerous assassins, must not escape. He asks again for prayers and,
seizing one more chance for mayhem, persuades Cuwaert and
Belijn to accompany him all the way home. Because of their
saintliness, he avers, they will sustain him spiritually. Cuwaert
is the prey he really wants, but the hare would probably refuse
without a protective chaperon. As we will shortly see, Belijn is
also gullible enough to become a victim.

When the three arrive at Manpertuus, Reinaert requests the
ram, whom he wheedles with the epithet "nephew," to have
Cuwaert come inside and console Hermeline. The hare feels safe
about going into the burrow since Belijn tells him to, even though
the ram must remain outside, being too large. Perhaps Cuwaert
thinks he earned Reinaert's gratitude by cooperating in regard
to Kriekeput. The pilgrim adds reassurance, moreover, so that
his former pupil is utterly seduced, like Arnout's Cantecleer.
Reinaert is able to accomplish in Willem's continuation what
Renart, who intends to feed Couart to his whelps, fails to bring
off in *Branche* I. Lest Hermeline have any scruples about eating
their guest, her husband alleges that Nobel has given them Cuwaert because the hare was the first to complain about him.
Willem may have forgotten that Isengrijn was the first and that
Cuwaert never complained at all, but then lying is second nature
with the fox. As the hare screams for help, Reinaert does what

Pancer the beaver prevented him from doing three days earlier; he bites Cuwaert's head off.

Hermeline's gratitude to Nobel for such a fine meal prompts her mate to explain that the king will soon be angry again. Eventually Nobel will learn that he has been deceived, Reinaert implies; Bruun and Isengrijn will help to educate him, for example. Varying the exile motif from *Branche* I, the fox therefore proposes moving to a wilderness of which he knows, where there is game aplenty but no vengeful society. He says he endured too much apprehension during his ordeal at court to risk putting himself at Nobel's mercy again, even though it is clear that he enjoyed hoodwinking his enemies. When Hermeline reminds him of his commitment to journey overseas, he sneers that he has no intention of fulfilling his vow. The pilgrimage would be to no avail anyway, he snorts, since he has ransomed himself with nothing more than a figment of his imagination. He does not deny being excommunicated, in spite of the fact that Arnout did not have him include the ban in his confession to Grimbeert.

By this time Belijn is beginning to call impatiently for Cuwaert, so the fox goes out to pull the wool over his eyes. The ram should return to court without the hare, barks Reinaert, for Cuwaert wants to comfort his "aunt" Hermeline and the children a little longer. In answer to Belijn's question about the cry for help, the fox contends that his wife fainted at the news of his pilgrimage. Having disposed of the hare, Reinaert now craves whatever injury he can inflict on the ram. As Renart jeers at Noble directly toward the end of *Branche* I, furthermore, so Reinaert conceives a way of taunting the king indirectly, with the unwitting aid of Uriah-like Belijn. He asks his "nephew," as he once more unctuously terms the ram, to take a couple of letters to Nobel in the satchel provided by Bruun, assuring Belijn that the lion would be grateful. Since the chaplain, who has fallen out of favor with his ruler, is delighted at this chance to make amends, Reinaert hangs the pouch with Cuwaert's head in it around his neck, warning that he must not look inside. He is welcome to claim credit for the contents, however, the fox concludes. After jumping with childish joy, Belijn trots off eagerly.

Having wreaked havoc in Nobel's kingdom, Reinaert leads his family toward that Eden he announced to Hermeline, where he will live like his fabled frogs before they stupidly invoked an overlord. It is a final inconsistency between Arnout's work and Willem's that voluntary exile is an option in the latter but not in the former. Back when Grimbeert came to Manpertuus with the third summons, Reinaert decided to heed it because he and his family would otherwise perish. In Texts A and L, if not also F, he even stated that he could not escape the king (line 1405 of A), yet escape the king is exactly what Willem has him do. How appropriate that Nobel's sway declines with his integrity! Captive to a good lion, Reinaert can elude a bad one.

In accordance with *Branche* I, Willem concludes the struggle between loner and group again in victory for the latter. Like Renart, Reinaert runs for his life, yet he does so at his leisure and without being harmed at all. The placid manner of his flight underscores his greater ability. More like the title figure in the Middle-High-German poem *Reinhart Fuchs,* who magisterially crumbles the upper crust, even poisoning Vrevel the lion with impunity, Willem's fox towers over other beasts in terms of talent, but ultimately his success is no greater than Renart's. Though he prevails in any one-on-one situation, where even the monarch is no match for him, his individual prowess cannot offset the collective power of mental dwarfs.

The extent to which he does play hob with the establishment reflects his author's grudge against it. Thus Willem resembles the author of *Branche* I, except that he resented society's impositions. As evidence of such vexation, Reinaert says to Hermeline, when introducing the idea of a move (lines 3148–50), "I hope that within two days I won't have to bother with Nobel's summons any more than he'd have to bother with mine." Willem continued Arnout's poem in order to express his ire at encroachments on his liberty, by people he considered as inferior to himself as the court is to his fox. What most appealed to him about *Proto-Reinaert* and *Branche* I both was surely their protagonists' recalcitrance, which he admired as a declaration of independence. Perhaps he would even have liked for his fox to be another Reinhart, assassinating Nobel, but he was too realistic. Instead of defeating the system which Arnout defended, he vicariously deserted it, though discrediting it first. For Reinaert not to leave would be perilous, of course, but exile means much more to him than safety. It offers a degree of freedom that exists only outside the body politic.

Willem's sequel may well have ended at line 3329, as the emigrants set out for their new home. We will see in the following section of this chapter that the final 140 lines of *Van den Vos Reynaerde* deal exclusively with the situation at court and focus on a radically different hero, while we have learned already that Willem's interest was in the fox. Where Reinaert's story stops is probably where Willem's writing stopped. A conclusion at line 3329 would leave unanswered the question of how Nobel reacts to Cuwaert's head and of the consequences for Belijn, but we can guess that the lion is mortified, and the fate of a minor figure like the ram matters little. Isengrijn and Bruun will naturally be released. Willem's termination at line 3329, like Arnout's at line 1885, was nonetheless sufficiently abrupt to provoke an extension.

It is also true that when Belijn jumps for joy outside Manpertuus Manuscripts A and F contain a reference to what befalls him after line 3329. "So happy was he over something that turned out badly for him," both texts read in regard to the leap (lines 3294–95 of A). This anticipatory remark is poor evidence that Willem wrote the last 140 lines, however, because it does not specify in what way Belijn's expectations will be soured, thus telling us nothing more than we would assume anyway. Its absence from *Reynardus Vulpes* and *Reinaerts Historie* suggests that it could even be a copyist's later insertion.

The Denouement

Belijn returns to court shortly after noon, carrying the bearhide satchel, into which he has obediently refrained from peeping. Reinaert gave it to him, he explains to Nobel, so he could bring a couple of letters, which he himself composed, as he proudly boasts. The king has him give the pouch to Botsaert the clerk,

who handles all mail. Botsaert (or Bockart in Manuscript F) is
said to be an ape in *Reynardus Vulpes,* where his name is Boccardus.
Although he has a major function at court, being the royal sec-
retary, he has not been previously mentioned, either in *Proto-
Reinaert* or in Willem's continuation. Together with Bruneel,
whom Arnout included among the fox's accusers (line 1857) and
who in Manuscript F is an otter, Botsaert removes the satchel
from Belijn's neck, discovering Cuwaert's head. "Help! What
kind of letter is this?" the ape exclaims, but it does convey a
message. After bowing his head in silent remorse, Nobel roars
like his counterpart in *Branche* I, terrifying everybody.

At this point we meet the leopard Firapeel (mistakenly called
Syrapeel in Manuscript A),[33] the lion's distant relative. Despite
the prominence he is to assume in this last section of *Van den Vos
Reynaerde,* where he replaces Gente as her husband's intimate
adviser,[34] he has been as unheard-of as Botsaert in the parts we
have ascribed to Arnout and Willem. Relying on his kinship to
prevent him from giving offense, Firapeel politely chides the king
for lack of self-control. Nobel is behaving as if the queen were
dead, he says. When the lion tries to justify his histrionics by
pointing out that Reinaert has caused him to dishonor himself
through the abuse of his formerly staunch supporters Bruun and
Isengrijn, Firapeel urges that His Majesty set about righting the
wrongs committed. The wolf and the bear must be freed and,
together with Hersuint, consoled by being allowed to devour
Belijn, who deserves to die for betraying Cuwaert. After the three
mistreated friends have been appeased, the court should capture
Reinaert and hang him without another trial, Firapeel continues,
unaware that the fox is now beyond their reach.

Apparently no one thinks the ram deserves a hearing, even
though his admission of guilt is highly suspicious. Why, after
all, would he want to be credited with murdering the hare? Is
it not clear that he has been tricked like the king? These questions
are never asked, even by Belijn, and the fact that he is a priest
in Willem's continuation is overlooked, for such considerations
would ruin the etiological fable which the author of the denouement sought to create, feeling that it would be cute to use the

situation left by Willem for an explanation of why wolves and bears kill sheep. The fact that this fairy-tale element is highly forced, contravening normal behavior, is evidence in itself that the poem's last 140 lines were not produced by Willem, who was too astute an observer of psychology to sacrifice it for some special effect.

Whereas Manuscript F concludes with the leopard's proposals, the other texts (A, L, and B) proceed. Nobel sighs that he would certainly be relieved if his kinsman's advice were carried out, so Firapeel unties Bruun and Isengrijn, apologizing for their plight. Provided they forgive the king and pledge allegiance, he will grant them Belijn and the ram's whole family as legal prey forever, the leopard promises. They may also molest Reinaert and all the fox's clan, Firapeel adds, abandoning already his idea of attacking Manpertuus. Nobel's peace, essential to *Proto-Reinaert* but never mentioned in Willem's continuation, is clearly forgotten in the denouement, even if the leopard's intention is not to include the likes of Grimbeert among the fox's relatives.

In the last eight lines (3462–69) of Manuscript A, Bruun and Isengrijn accept the offer extended by Firapeel, uniting the court in blissful solidarity. Balduinus, the author of *Reynardus Vulpes,* also has the wolf and the bear accept the royal offer, but not so quickly. In a short passage (lines 1795–1800 of Text L)[35] equivalent to the final eight lines of Manuscript A, Brunus and Ysengrinus consult their families before acquiescing and then formally confirm their agreement in King Leo's presence. The corresponding lines (3467–68) in *Reinaerts Historie* state merely, "Thus was peace restored by Firapeel the leopard."

Balduinus's account of the reconciliation probably reproduces the original conclusion of the denouement to *Van den Vos Reynaerde. Reynardus Vulpes* antedates all extant vernacular versions of the poem, and the first letter in each of the final nine lines of Manuscript A almost form the acrostic *BI WILLEME* ("BY WILLEM"). Perhaps taking a cue from line 3461 of A, which begins with *Bi Gode* ("By God"), an enterprising copyist seems to have rewritten the lines that followed so as to close with an artistic flourish, attributing the whole poem to the man who claims its authorship in the prologue. Unfortunately, however, a still later scribe overlooked the acrostic and spoiled it by changing lines 3464–65, which no longer commence with the proper letters.

While merely tying up loose ends, the last contributor to *Van den Vos Reynaerde* was still able to weave his own design into a fabric already composed of two clashing patterns. In contrast to Arnout and Willem, who used Reynard material to express antithetical views of law and order, he seized upon it for the glorification of competent courtiers. The denouement is dominated neither by the king nor by the rebel, those principal antagonists in both *Proto-Reinaert* and Willem's continuation, but rather by a practical, energetic couselor. Firapeel is a kind of Fortinbras, says Arendt,[36] and indeed the leopard concludes *Van den Vos Reynaerde* by filling a political vacuum. Nobel does not die, but he might as well, for he is reduced to a figurehead, dependent on subordinates. Nobody will ever know who the author of the final 140 lines was, but his high opinion of officials implies that he was of their number. Like Arnout he identified with the establishment, for he carefully rebuilt what Willem had contemptuously shattered.

The Prologue

Now that we are acquainted with the body of *Van den Vos Reynaerde,* we can better understand its first forty lines, which also bear the marks of more than one creator. That prefatory section really consists of two different prologues—the initial ten lines, clearly composed by Willem, and the next thirty, which Arnout must have penned.

Willem introduces himself in lines 1–2 as the author of a work entitled *Madoc.*[37] This bit of information, along with the fact that he at least contributed to the composition of *Van den Vos Reynaerde,* is all we really know about Willem, and *Madoc* has not survived. In lines 3–9 Willem claims to have been irked that Arnout's story about Reinaert was left incomplete,[38] so he looked up French accounts of the fox and began rendering them into Dutch. Although *Proto-Reinaert* is much more a translation from

French than is the part of *Van den Vos Reynaerde* which we have attributed to Willem, we have noted probable influence on his contribution from several *branches* of the *Roman de Renart* (Ia, VI, and X, as well as I), and what a medieval author alleges about his sources must be taken with a grain of salt. It is a convention of older literature that supposed authenticity took precedence over originality, which was to be obscured by the pretense of repeating someone else's "history." In his tenth line Willem is also quite conventional, calling upon God for help, and such an invocation forms a natural conclusion for a prologue, even if from the hollow quill of an evident atheist. Willem does not explicitly state that he is completing what he thought was Arnout's fragmentary poem, but he implies as much, after clearly documenting the existence of an earlier Reynard epic in Dutch.

Whereas Willem wrote his ten-line introduction in the third-person singular, Arnout couched lines 11–40 in the first-person singular. It is true that in Manuscripts A and B the tenth line shifts to "us" (while Manuscript F keeps the third person here—"May God grant him His help"), but we find a change at line eleven in any case. Though this is a small consideration, for such variations in person occur in many medieval prologues, it harmonizes with the other evidence for double authorship of *Van den Vos Reynaerde*'s preface.

"Now I am concerned here at the outset that clods and fools who listen to this poem, which will be lost on them, might find fault with it," Arnout begins. (It is their reaction to an explicit hanging of the fox that he may have feared. See page 85.) Such people, he declares, are often so opinionated that they misconstrue literature, about which they are as ignorant as he professes to be in regard to Babylonians. "I don't say that for my sake," he states, explaining, "I wouldn't have composed this tale about Reinaert if I hadn't been asked to do so by a lady fond of courtliness." Although he chides carping clods and fools, Arnout continues, he wants those gentlefolk to hear his narrative who care for honor and propriety, be they rich or poor. Rather than terminate with a prayer for divine assistance (something which would have been more appropriate for him than for Willem but which he may have considered ostentatious), Arnout simply announces that the story will now commence. He rounded his prologue off, making it rhetorically a unit, by setting the same word, *Nu* ("Now"), at the start of both its first and its last lines.

Willem gives dissatisfaction with an earlier work as his motive for writing, while Arnout claims to be responding to a benefactress's plea. The nature of *Proto-Reinaert* indicates why Arnout was apprehensive about being misinterpreted. It champions the civilized behavior of Nobel's retinue, just as Arnout's putative patroness desired, but his fox might be admired, not reprehended. Perhaps because of the vogue Renart enjoyed, the lady fond of courtliness (or Arnout himself, if she is his invention) wanted a Flemish poem about the fox which would be as interesting as *Branche* I and yet uphold decorum.

Not only does the assertion of a different reason for creating a Reynard epic argue that Willem did not compose lines 11–40, but that passage is also shrilly out of keeping with his exaltation of antisocial actions. He would have to have been improbably ironic to have written (lines 34–37), "I want those people to listen who gladly pursue honor and are concerned to live politely. . . ." The likeliest explanation is that Willem both extended *Proto-Reinaert* and, instead of replacing Arnout's prologue, merely prefixed his own to it. That he would leave Arnout's intact, despite its incompatibility with his, suggests, like the other inconsistencies we have noticed, that Willem also did not alter the body of Arnout's poem. Except for slight changes introduced by copyists, lines 11–1885 of *Van den Vos Reynaerde,* as it exists in Manuscript A, still constitute the original *Proto-Reinaert.*

Composition Dates

There is no clearly identifiable reference in *Van den Vos Reynaerde* to any historic event or personage that can serve as a foothold for determining composition dates, even though some scholars have argued to the contrary, and we do not know when Arnout or Willem lived. A *terminus ad quem* would be Balduinus's Latin translation, which dates from 1272–79,[39] but *Proto-Reinaert* may well have originated around 1200. In any case, Willem must have added his continuation not more than about ten years later, with the denouement appended fairly soon after that.[40] The fact that Willem mentions Arnout without identifying him implies that Willem was writing at a time not far removed from the composition date of *Proto-Reinaert,* when listeners could still be expected to know who Arnout was. If there had been a long interval between the production of the first and second stages of *Van den Vos Reynaerde,* Willem himself would hardly have known about Arnout. The absence of any *Proto-Reinaert* manuscript per se and of any *Van-den-Vos-Reynaerde* text without at least part of the denouement also leads one to believe that the successive steps in the evolution of the work took place rather quickly. Each stage, seeming more nearly complete than the previous one, supplanted the earlier version before many copies of it had been made.

Regardless of the anticlimactic conclusion with its contrived etiology, the sometimes jarring disharmony between Arnout's and Willem's contributions, and the latter's shaky start, *Van den Vos Reynaerde* is the most exciting of all the Reynard epics, thanks primarily to what we might call the Satanic charisma of Willem's hero, in whom his brilliant contemporary, Emperor Frederick II, would have recognized a kindred spirit. *Reinaerts Historie,* which adds much more material to the conflict between fox and society begun by the author of *Branche* I, has traditionally been rated far below *Van den Vos Reynaerde* as a work of art. To what extent its inferior reputation is deserved, the next chapter will show.

Chapter Four
Reinaerts Historie

Early in the Great Schism, around 1380,[1] an unknown contemporary of Chaucer from either Flanders or the province of Holland did to *Van den Vos Reynaerde* what Willem had done to *Proto-Reinaert*. He appended a continuation in which the fox's fortunes are vastly improved. The new extension is much longer than Willem's, however, for in Ernst Martin's critical edition (note 1 to this chapter) *Reinaerts Historie* numbers 7,794 verses. Whereas Willem seems not to have changed *Proto-Reinaert*, moreover, the fourteenth-century author largely rewrote *Van den Vos Reynaerde* before proceeding to his sequel, although only a few of his alterations are important. We will examine the most significant ones in our following section, while some lesser modifications that are still worthy of attention were pointed out either in the body of the previous chapter or in footnotes to it.[2]

Major Changes in *Van den Vos Reynaerde*

As the author indicates at the end of *Reinaerts Historie,* the purpose of his epic is to warn against a moral climate favorable to smooth-talking but self-seeking courtiers, epitomized by the fox. Our latest Reinaert is therefore neither Arnout's psychopath nor Willem's aspirant to total freedom but a negative version of Firapeel. At least as valuable as the leopard on account of his astute judgment, he is nonetheless more harmful than helpful because he looks out for his own best interests instead of the king's.

In order to portray Reinaert as a dangerous politician, who ceases to be the outsider of *Branche* I, *Proto-Reinaert,* and Willem's continuation, becoming very much an insider, the *Historie*'s author had to bring him back to court. Since to do so from exile would have been almost impossible, the author removed expatriation from his recasting of *Van den Vos Reynaerde*. Instead of acquiescing in her husband's proposal to flee, Hermeline convinces him that at home they are fairly secure, even though their burrow is still not impregnable. If perchance it were taken, she argues, they could slip out one of the many back doors with which Manpertuus (called Malpertuus in Martin's text of the *Historie*) has been provided (lines 3183–99). When Bruun brings the first summons in the revision, fifteen lines (565–79) are inserted, describing the den as long, narrow, and crooked, with secret entrances on all sides, through which its occupants can sneak in or out unseen. Because his abode is safer in the *Historie* than in *Van den Vos Reynaerde,* the fox can remain there, available for another trial.

By the same token, of course, it is not so necessary for him to go to court initially in *Reinaerts Historie* as it was in *Van den Vos Reynaerde,* where a refusal would have spelled catastrophe for his whole family. In the later work he heeds Grimbeert's (now Grimbaert's) citation in order to keep his wife and children from worrying (lines 1436–41). He is sure, moreover, that he can reinstate himself in the king's good graces on account of his indispensable advice. The court cannot function without him (lines 1411–29). The clear implication is thus that the Nobel of *Reinaerts Historie* is so dependent on the fox as to be easily inclinable in his favor—a circumstance of great importance for the outcome of Reinaert's second trial.

Another highly influential factor on that occasion will be the fox's kinsmen. We noted at the very beginning of Willem's continuation of *Proto-Reinaert* that Nobel was momentarily shaken by the walkout which Grimbeert started, so that in *Van den Vos Reynaerde* the fox's relatives already had some effect on the king, however negligible. In *Reinaerts Historie* the fox's clan is much more prominent as a political power, and we will see that the pressure it exerts on Nobel decisively affects his treatment of its acknowledged leader.

To strengthen the solidarity of that shady clan, the author of
the *Historie* refashioned Grimbeert's personality. The badger who
had been devout, honest, and well intentioned became his uncle's
devious accomplice. We begin to perceive that his uprightness
is specious when he first fetches Reinaert from Malpertuus. Two
cynical lines (1404–1405) are added to his speech advising the
fox to heed Nobel's summons. The gist of them is that Reinaert
knows enough dirty tricks to save himself.[3] By offering such
encouragement, the new Grimbeert implies that he is not averse
to immorality.

His readiness to support questionable and even criminal behavior by Reinaert (and by the latter's sons, as we will see) means
that his role as father confessor, which the author of the *Historie*
preserved from *Van den Vos Reynaerde,* becomes part of the sacrilegious comedy staged by the fox. The badger reduces his re-
quirements for absolution, but he does not thereby mock true
penance overtly. He still lectures his uncle on proper conduct,
and when Reinaert lunges toward the nuns' rooster at the com-
pletion of the confession, Grimbaert rails just as angrily as Arnout's Grimbeert (lines 1732–63).[4]

In contrast to these innovations, a final one included in the
rewriting of *Van den Vos Reynaerde* is unacceptable. Instead of
separating themselves from the fox by going to the gallows,
Bruun, Isengrijn (or Isegrijn), and Tibeert take Reinaert with
them, and everyone else tags along (lines 2012–31). The bear,
the wolf, and the cat should therefore be able to hear how they
supposedly plotted against the king, yet somehow they do not.
Tiecelijn the crow must still inform them of what the fox has
said (lines 2799–2811), the *Historie*'s author having evidently
forgotten that he had moved the court to the gibbet. In his sequel
to *Van den Vos Reynaerde* we will discover some further errors but
fortunately none of such magnitude.

Before taking up the continuation, we need to become acquainted with the work on which it is based—1542-line *Branche*
VI of the *Roman de Renart.* As in Chapter Two, we will follow
Martin's edition.[5] *Branche* VI, like the somewhat earlier X, was
composed as a merely entertaining substitute for *Branche* I, though

without providing a direct account of how or why Renart is brought to court. Many complaints against him, including three manqué attempts to summon him, are described in retrospect, but the poem commences when he arrives at the royal palace with Grimbert, who has just been sent as the fourth envoy to fetch him. (The legal tradition of three citations at most is therefore ignored, or overlooked.)[6]

Branche VI of the *Roman de Renart*

For three days the lion has been holding court, and all his barons have arrived except the fox, who fears hostility. Because the king desires a joyful atmosphere, the scene is noisy, as drums are rapped and voices raised in song. The author of VI was probably thinking of *Branche* X, which also opens festively. Grimbert ends the merriment at line 28, however, by darkening the palace door with his baleful relative.

Initially apprehensive, Renart pulls himself together and kneels with a show of confidence, after being encouraged by the badger. In *Branche* I he delivers a complacent address before Noble scolds him; but in VI that order is reversed, while the gist of both speeches remains quite similar. In each *branche* the lion threatens to punish the fox, who argues that he is a maligned and unappreciated servant, although he concludes in VI with an example of his self-sacrifice. He reminds Noble of how he allegedly journeyed to Rome, Salerno, and Montpellier for medicine when the king was sick (an allusion to *Branche* X). Noble counters with a long review of offenses perpetrated by the fox against Tibert, Brun, the titmouse, Copee, Tiecelin, and Hersent, essentially as we know them from *Branches* I and II-Va, plus malevolence toward the dog Roonel à la X. (Renart misled Roonel, who subpoenaed him, much like the bear and the cat.)

The fox stays calm under fire, silently bowing his head. He also requests permission to speak before repeating that he has been falsely incriminated and that he deserves better for his services. Even though his victims protest his hypocrisy, he swears that he cannot recall having ever sinned against them. To strengthen the impression of purity he is trying to convey, he

declares that he is willing to vindicate himself either by an ordeal
(like Hersent in *Branche* I) or in a duel.

Noble yields to Ysengrin, who has a much larger part to play
in VI than in I. (The authors of both VI and X were dissatisfied
with his meager role in I.) He testifies that he saw the fox assault
his wife. As in *Branche* II-Va, however, Renart insists that what
at a distance looked like abuse was only a well-meaning attempt
to dislodge Hersent from Malpertuis's entrance. She herself must
not be on hand to contradict him, for we do not hear from her
and her presence at court is never indicated.

Stymied in his effort to prove Renart guilty of rape, Ysengrin
summarizes five pranks which the fox has played on him. Though
he makes some changes, we can recognize the descent into the
well from *Branche* IV, the ice fishing and the tonsuring from
Branche III, along with the drunken mass (altered to a less impious
carousal in a wine cellar, as suggested by *Ysengrimus*) and the
encounter with fishmongers from *Branche* XIV. Ysengrin begins
the series with the well and pond incidents, which he links
together as two fishing trips. Renart blames their painful consequences on the wolf's own greed and takes the opportunity to
preach a short, seven-line sermon on the theme of "whoever covets
everything loses everything,"[7] giving the impression that he,
more than Ysengrin, is the champion of morality. He ascribes
to the wolf's intoxication the beating received in the wine cellar,
and he dismisses as untrue the last two misadventures described
by Ysengrin. They are the tonsuring and the frustrated trickery
of the merchants, which the wolf construes as having both resulted
from his hunger for eels, exploited by Renart.

Unable to obtain a conviction through argument, Ysengrin
decides in desperation to seize upon the fox's earlier suggestion
of a duel. Equity can only be acquired through combat in this
case. Renart accepts the wolf's challenge, for he considers himself
a skilled fighter and evidently does not believe that divine justice
will intervene, as medieval theory presupposed. To refuse, moreover, would be interpreted as cowardice if not as a tacit admission
of guilt. After Brun, Tibert, Chantecler, and Couart have been
selected as pledges for Ysengrin, along with Grimbert, Baucent

the boar, Espinart the hedgehog, and Belin for Renart, Noble announces that the battle will take place in two weeks. Until then court is adjourned.

Armed with a shield and a staff as their weapon, the gladiators return at the appointed time, Renart having shaved his head and neck. His family remains at home, praying for him. So does Hersent, for she cherishes the "sweet" way he ravished her and resents her husband's public complaint. Named judge of the duel, Brichemer the stag chooses the leopard, plus Baucent (even though the boar is dedicated to Renart) and Bruyant the bull to assist him. On Brichemer's initiative the four ask Noble for permission to seek a peaceful settlement. The king approves, but Ysengrin refuses to be reconciled, so that the match, *Branche* VI's contribution to Reynard literature, can finally begin.

Just as the fox was required to swear his innocence on the "relic" Roonel in II-Va, so must both he and the wolf take a sacred oath here, though in *Branche* VI no trickery is involved. The remains of a genuine saint are brought by Belin, who is now a chaplain, as we noted in Chapter Three. Supervised by Brichemer and Brun, Renart vows that he is blameless, while Ysengrin swears that his foe is committing perjury. Like the fox setting out for court in *Branche* I, the wolf prays for vengeance. Renart would invoke help through a magic charm but has forgotten too much of the necromancy he learned in his youth. Although the author tells us that the fox is eager for combat because he has mastered all appropriate feints, Renart begs off, promising to do homage to his adversary and pilgrimage in the latter's behalf if acquitted without a fight. Ysengrin is less disposed to accommodate the fox, whom he does not even believe, than Brichemer, however.

Renart deals the first blow, and it is to the head, stunning the wolf, but Ysengrin still refuses a truce, which the fox again requests. Renart then breaks Ysengrin's left arm. Without their shields but continuing to wield a stick, the two begin to wrestle, and the wounded wolf is thrown. Jumping on him, the fox beats him in the face, breaking some of his teeth, and throws dust into his eyes while also spitting at him and pulling his whiskers.

Renart even blows his nose into Ysengrin's face. In despair the wolf curses women as the worst of all evils, since it is primarily on account of his wife that he is suffering so, but at this point the tide of battle turns. If divine justice does not object to Renart's unsportsmanlike conduct, in *Branche* VI (unlike *Reinaerts Historie*) it certainly will not permit a perjurer to win. For no apparent reason the fox loses his cudgel, and as he grabs for Ysengrin's eyes, a finger slips into the wolf's mouth. Crunching it to the bone, Ysengrin is able to roll over on top of Renart, whom he pins with his knees and pummels into unconsciousness. His prayer for revenge has been answered.

Noble even orders Renart to be hung, as in *Branche* I, but the author of VI, in contrast to Arnout, would not depart far enough from tradition to let the fox actually die. In *Branche* I Renart is freed under the proviso that he become a pilgrim; in VI he is required to become a monk,[8] being released in the custody of Brother Bernart,[9] who takes him to the fraternity at Grandmont. Eventually he is expelled for eating capons and a crow, so that he can again plague Ysengrin, but he goes home first, to be welcomed by his family as in *Branches* XIV and I.

Like *Branche* VI, the sequel to *Van den Vos Reynaerde* consists mainly of debate but also of judicial combat. In the course of the litigation, furthermore, the fox protects himself with lies, as in *Branche* VI, and episodes from his past are recounted. The author of the *Historie* did not follow *Branche* VI closely, however, for he also included material from other sources, along with much of his own making.

The Continuation of *Van den Vos Reynaerde*

Although the *Historie* contains no breaks at all, its second half is best divided into four parts, as determined by structure. Each of the first three comprises accusations against the fox and his defense, while by and large the fourth is devoted to a duel between him and Isegrijn. The charges will form an inverse chronological sequence, since those occasioned by Reinaert's most recent misdeeds are brought first and complaints about his oldest wrongs come last.

Part One: Verses 3481–4644. At the end of *Van den Vos
Reynaerde,* as revised by the *Historie*'s author, Nobel prolongs the
meeting of his court for twelve days in honor of Bruun and
Isegrijn, who have been exonerated of treason. For this reason the
sequel to *Van den Vos Reynaerde* begins very much like *Branche*
VI. Everyone is rejoicing, and any creatures not present before,
or any who left during Reinaert's trial, like the badger,[10] have
arrived to swell the music and dancing—except for the fox, of
course. Again he is afraid to attend, and with particularly good
reason now, though he does not scruple to continue the lawless
trickery which has jeopardized him. After the royal festival has
lasted a week, it is abruptly terminated by the entrance of Lampreel the rabbit, with four gashes in his head and one ear missing.

The regal couple and their immediate attendants are having
lunch when Lampreel staggers before them. The previous day,
he sobs, while passing Malpertuus on the way to court, he met
Reinaert dressed as a pilgrim and praying. Without uttering a
word, the dissembler bared his claws, and the rabbit was lucky
to survive. When Lampreel completes his report he causes a minor
inconsistency by announcing that he sees Corbout the crow and
the latter's wife Scerpenebbe bringing a similar grievance. Corbout does indeed flutter down with another serious charge against
the fox, but his lament is that Reinaert has murdered Scerpenebbe. Just a few hours earlier, Corbout squawks, he and his
mate found the pretender lying as if dead. While investigating,
Scerpenebbe came too close to Reinaert's open jaws and was
beheaded.

After commencing chiefly with the help of *Branche* VI, the
Historie's author departed from that source in order to provide his
badger with a fresh, dramatic reason for fetching the fox and to
make the eventual reversal of Reinaert's status even more im-
pressive than it would be if the fox did not continue misbehaving.
The mutilation of Lampreel combines the wounding of Cuwaert
as described by Pancer the beaver with Cantecleer's account of
Reinaert as a pilgrim in Arnout's poem, and the killing of Scerpenebbe—a pendant to the slaying of Coppe—could be copied
from *Branches* XIII and XVII of the *Roman de Renart,* where the

fox decoys crows in much the same way.[11] The accusations brought by Lampreel and Corbout rekindle the king's anger at Reinaert, forcing another confrontation. The primary function of this whole first part of the continuation is in fact to start a second trial against the fox. Reinaert's particular task in Part Two will be to regain the royal favor which Willem had him scout, while in the remaining sections of the sequel he must triumph over Isegrijn, his bitterest enemy. Only then can his success be maximized.

The author has him accused of attempted homicide prior to actual murder because double crimes of increasing magnitude are likely to have a stronger effect on Nobel than only a single felony would. That the lion roars with rage, as in *Branche* I and the denouement to *Van den Vos Reynaerde,* frightening everyone, does not surprise us. What really irks him, as also in the denouement to *Van den Vos Reynaerde,* is having been gulled himself by the fox, although he blames that deception on his wife, and he asks the court to help restore his honor by stopping Reinaert's outrages.

Isegrijn and Bruun are certainly willing, but only the queen dares speak at this juncture, and she disagrees with her husband. Beginning in French and including a correct Latin quotation,[12] she warns against rashness. Her advice is that the fox be allowed a rebuttal. After all, she observes, he is a wise counselor and the head of a mighty clan. Because of these two factors, she implies, Reinaert must be granted special consideration. Firapeel joins her in urging moderation, and even Isegrijn concurs, being sure that the fox will have to forfeit his life for other transgressions, if he can clear himself of Lampreel's and Corbout's indictments. The wolf does not yet specify what those other transgressions are, but he denounces Reinaert's yarn about the treasure at Kriekeput and the conspiracy. Dissuaded from precipitate action, Nobel gives the fox six days in which to appear. Since Reinaert will not be summoned, Grimbaert decides to alert his uncle.

On the way to Malpertuus he is anxious over the threat to the leader of his family, until he remembers the fox's cleverness. Reinaert will win at court, the badger concludes (lines 3772–73), thanks to superb skill in lying. Thus Grimbaert confirms that cynicism we found initially revealed during his first trip to Malpertuus, as described in the *Historie*. Far from condemning or regretting his uncle's mendacity, he rejoices over it. When he reaches the den, he nervously imparts his news, but Reinaert is not perturbed. The fox feels that he is indispensable to the government, so that again we find an idea repeated from the badger's earlier visit.

In what immediately follows, the author of the *Historie* borrowed from both *Branche* I and *Van den Vos Reynaerde*. Grimbaert dines and spends the night at Malpertuus, like Grimbert at Malpertuis, but instead of making another confession at home, Reinaert waits until he and the badger are once more on the road.

After dinner the fox extols the deftness of his cubs Rosseel and Reinaerdijn in the sinister art of catching game. Like him, he says, they seduce their prey with friendliness. Grimbaert further shows his own lack of true virtue by congratulating Reinaert on such capable sons. The badger is proud of his kinship with the little hoodlums. Everyone goes to bed, but the fox lies awake, brooding over a way to save himself, just as he plotted a course of action during the night before his first trial, according to what Willem wrote.

At dawn on the second day of our new story he and his nephew leave Malpertuus. Hermeline reminds him in vain of his intention, never again to be at Nobel's mercy. He is not apprehensive now, apparently being satisfied that the odds are in his favor, on account of his defense and his value as a counselor. (He does not yet know whether he can count on his kinfolk's support.) As before, he is better off gambling at court than at home, even though the latter remains a valid option for him, and gamboling in exile was just a passing whim.

En route to the palace he wants to acknowledge his naughtiness again, or to have it acknowledged by his junior partner. Since he was last shriven he has lied to Nobel, arranged to have Bruun, Isegrijn, the she-wolf Eerswinde, and Belijn mistreated, and has directly assaulted Cuwaert, Lampreel, and Scerpenebbe, Reinaert relates. He does not include the fact that he took liberties with

Grimbaert's good name by implicating his nephew in his imagined conspiracy, and the badger ignores that peccadillo, too, if
he even knows of it. Since we are already familiar with the
misdeeds which the fox does mention, he passes over them
quickly, devoting the bulk of his conscience cleansing to the
detailed recollection of an earlier sin against Isegrijn, forgotten
on the former hike to court.

He describes how the wolf told him, as they chanced upon a
mare with her foal one day, to ask whether she would sell the
little fellow. Not without a sense of humor, she declared that
the price was inscribed under her right foot, if Reinaert cared to
look. He warily excused himself on the grounds of illiteracy,
whereupon Isegrijn, boasting a mastery of French, Dutch, and
Latin, bounded over, to be kicked senseless. Reinaert observed
that the most educated people are often not the wisest.

Thus the author edifies us with a fable—the first of many
which he worked into his sequel. It derives from the *Romulus*
tale, noted in connection with Nivardus's kick episode, about a
lion and a horse, but no source is known that contains a mare
and the same moral. Such a lack is puzzling, since the miller
Simkin says in lines 134–35 of Chaucer's "Reeve's Tale," " 'The
gretteste clerkes been noght the wysest men,' / As whylom to
the wolf thus spak the mare."

A possible explanation is that Chaucer, whose wife Philippa
was the daughter of a knight from Henegouwen, encountered
Reinaerts Historie before he wrote "The Reeve's Tale" and is alluding to the *Historie* in the lines just quoted. He can have shifted
the moral from Reinaert to the mare for the sake of rhyme, or
perhaps his memory was faulty. The *Historie*'s author can then
have borrowed from the French work *Renart le Contrefait,* the
earlier text of which (Manuscript A) was completed in 1322 and
contains a fairly similar anecdote, though without the moral. [13]
Flinn has suggested that the form of the tale in *Renart le Contrefait*
combines elements from the first and tenth stories in the collection titled *Fabulae Extravagantes.* [14]

When the confession has ended, Grimbaert bestows absolution
rather perfunctorily, even dispensing with penance under the

pretext that Reinaert is sufficiently troubled by guilt. The badger is impatient to express concern about his uncle's physical, instead of spiritual, well-being. The prank with Cuwaert's head and the dupery of Nobel have seriously jeopardized the fox, he remonstrates, and he means at court, not in heaven, because he refers to the sending of the gory token (line 4123) rather than to the hare's decapitation. Apparently he is not in the least disturbed about the wrongs involved; only about what he construes to have been tactical errors that cannot be corrected.

In replying, Reinaert does not really deal with the issues raised by his nephew, for they will furnish the substance of the continuation's second part. Instead, he justifies his mendacity—that trait in politicians which the *Historie*'s author wanted to stress above all others. To save himself the second time, the fox will again resort to lies, for which reason it is appropriate that he comment on his falseness, despite being false in doing so. In this instance falseness may be especially apt, but at any rate it implies that even with his confidant Reinaert strives to project a positive image. (The crimes he has described to Grimbaert of course redound to his credit with that shifty fellow traveler.)

He begins his 138-line disquisition on dishonesty by claiming that he is mystically at one with God when alone. Other creatures arouse his lusts, seducing him with pleasure, he continues, and they teach him to prevaricate, especially at court. There, to be honest means to run a great risk of failure, for only persuasive orators will be heeded, no matter how much they distort. Falsehoods per se do not guarantee success, however; they must be so cleverly delivered that the truth is less plausible. To help impress his nephew, Reinaert strikes a righteous pose by decrying speakers who lie for hire, as though they were really worse than the ones who lie only for personal advantage, like him. In conclusion he points out that everyone has to fib at times, because honesty can make life difficult. By admitting duplicity yet denying any blame for it, he demonstrates how ugly reality can be dressed in pretty words, and Grimbaert is enraptured.

Before long the two arrive at court. Even though many of his own kin are suspicious of him at this point, Reinaert acts un-

daunted, much as when he made his previous entrance, back in
Arnout's work. Like the badger in *Branche* VI, his nephew encourages him,[15] and he kneels before Nobel like the fox in that
branche. His initial comments to the king and the latter's response
are both to a great extent imitations of their lines at the commencement of the trial in *Proto-Reinaert*. With the warning that
creatures are not always what they seem (as he should know), the
fox pleads for an unbiased hearing and asserts that he has been
spitefully misrepresented by jealous rivals, on account of the royal
favor he has earned. Nobel is just as impatient with him as before,
rejecting his rhetoric and threatening him with death for breaking
the peace in his attacks on Lampreel and Scerpenebbe (who replace
Bruun and Tibeert from the corresponding speech at the first
trial).[16]

A second address by Reinaert, 261 lines long, is without
equivalent in any source. After an introduction in which he requests permission to defend himself because of his record as a
counselor, his loyalty, and his self-styled clear conscience, the fox
describes an encounter he pretends to have had with his uncle,
Mertijn the ape, a functionary of the Bishop of Cambrai at the
Roman Curia. Just after Grimbaert had brought news of Corbout's
and Lampreel's complaints, Reinaert avers, he met Mertijn out
on the heath.

Asked why he looked downcast, he explained that he had been
slandered by the rabbit in return for kindness. He had treated
Lampreel to lunch, which consisted of buttered pancakes, for he
was fasting devoutly in anticipation of Pentecost (even though
his first trial took place during Whitsuntide). When Rosseel
came to the table and reached for leftovers, Lampreel knocked
the young cub unconscious, whereupon Reinaerdijn avenged his
brother by mangling the rabbit. Reinaert claims to have told
Mertijn then of how Corbout flew up to report that Scerpenebbe
had died from eating too many maggots.

When the ape advised him to present at court the "true" version
of these two calamities, the fox continues, he informed his uncle
of the ban imposed by Herman, which makes him an outcast and
compels him to undertake a pilgrimage. Mertijn promised that

he would force Herman to withdraw the excommunication, Reinaert would have the court believe, and it seems that among the corrupt Roman clergy the ape has powerful relatives who can easily be bribed. Meanwhile, the fox declares, he has already been rehabilitated because Mertijn assumed the guilt which was incurred by urging Isegrijn to leave Elmare.

By way of coaxing his clan to support him, Reinaert maintains that the ape was sure of their readiness to help, and in particular he prods Mertijn's wife Rukenau, who is at court, by stating that his uncle especially recommended her. In parting, Mertijn allegedly threatened to have Nobel's kingdom interdicted at the fox's request. According to Reinaert, the ape related that he could arrange such retribution because the pope is guided by a young cardinal whose mistress is Mertijn's obedient niece. With this satire on the papacy at Rome the fantasy ends, and Reinaert concludes his whole address by welcoming any accusations which animals other than Corbout and Lampreel might be harboring. He will prove his innocence either through argument or combat, he boasts.

Since the rabbit and the crow have no confirmation of their charges against the fox, his explanation of what happened to them offsets theirs and necessitates his acquittal on those two counts. His reaffirmation of the Church's ban against him justifies his tardiness, furthermore, while the words imputed to Mertijn obviate his pilgrimage, now that he has no further use for it. Thus he accomplishes three important tasks with this longest speech of Part One. In addition, his appeal to Rukenau and the other relatives will have extremely valuable consequences for him in the second section of the sequel, and Nobel may actually be intimidated by Mertijn's putative threat of an interdict.

Reinaert's brazen self-assurance at the close of his discourse awes the court, and Part One terminates as Lampreel and Corbout admit defeat by slinking dispiritedly from sight, though they mutter a curse upon the "fell, false murderer," who proclaims his guile, they whisper, as if it were the gospel truth. By their testimony, therefore, Reinaert meets his own definition of a skill-

ful speaker, as set forth in the lecture to Grimbaert. His oratory
so far is only a warm-up, however, for what is to come.

Part Two: Verses 4645–6243. Nobel invites other complaints against the fox, and when none is raised, he himself damns
Reinaert on account of Cuwaert's head. "How could you be so
stupid as to dare insult me that way?" he thunders (expressing
more concern for his own image than for the hare's life). He goes
on to stress that the fox has no defense, because Belijn made a
complete confession, and that Reinaert, like the ram, will be put
to death.

Though complacent a moment before, the fox is thunderstruck
now. At a total loss for words, he gazes helplessly at his kin, but
they stare mutely back. We may well wonder how he can possibly
be so confounded after brooding all night over strategy and having
been reminded by Grimbaert of the danger incurred with Cuwaert's head. It looks as though the author, who wanted the fox's
clan to begin asserting its influence, could contrive no better way
for a family spokesman to intercede. The author may also have
been affected in this instance by *Branche* VI, where Renart hesitates with bowed head before replying to his king's indictment.
The French fox is only waiting for Noble to cool off, but Reinaert's
stupefaction superficially resembles Renart's politeness.

Dame Rukenau ends the embarrassing pause by responding to
her nephew's silent appeal for help, being also mindful, no doubt,
of the indirect solicitation included in his long Part-One speech.
She carries more weight than Grimbaert, to some extent because
of her husband, and the medieval mind associated apes more than
badgers with immorality. The *Historie*'s author probably considered her both a more influential and a more appropriate advocate
than Grimbaert. As an authority on law, she admonishes the lion
to remain a calm and impartial judge. Citing scripture, she also
exhorts him to be a sympathetic fellow mortal, since everyone
errs. Then she declares that Reinaert and his forebears have been
too valuable to the crown for him to be rejected in favor of his
enemies, Bruun and Isegrijn. Scoundrels are gaining control to
the detriment of wise and virtuous souls, she preaches, in a
reminiscence of what the fox said at the outset of his first trial.

Nobel doubts that she would champion Reinaert if he had troubled her as much as he has disturbed the realm. Except for her, the king opines, not even kith and kin are well disposed toward the nuisance. This retort challenges Rukenau to rally the clan around its traditional leader, particularly since Nobel seems to imply that his own attitude toward Reinaert is at least partly determined by public opinion.

Riveting the king's attention with six proverbs fired off in succession, the she-ape documents her nephew's value as a counselor by recounting an incident which harks back, directly or not, to the fifth tale in *Disciplina Clericalis.* [17] Two years before, a hungry dragon threatened to eat the man who had released it from a fence in which it had been caught. Reinaert, whom Nobel asked to arbitrate, recommended that the litigants reenact the original situation. Once the dragon was back in the fence, the fox advised the king not to intervene any further. Having reverted to the conditions which existed before their disagreement began, neither party had won or lost, and the man could choose whether to repeat his benefaction or not. For all practical purposes, of course, he had won completely, while the dragon had not only lost but had been sentenced to death by starvation. Nobel was satisfied that justice had been rendered, however. When has Bruun or Isegrijn, who care only about themselves, performed such service, Rukenau queries. Reinaert's contributions as a consultant are not really pertinent to the question of his guilt or innocence, but his aunt wants to divert attention from that issue, where he is weak, and direct it to his strengths.

In the remainder of her speech she stresses his political clout. She denies that Reinaert's relations repudiate him, as Nobel has implied, and she subtly threatens the king by declaring that anyone else who cast such an aspersion on the family would be chastised unforgettably. In order to impress on Nobel just what he has to contend with, she introduces the clan, thereby also renewing its loyalty. She starts with herself and sets an inspiring standard for the rest by pledging everything she has, including her life, to the fox's welfare. Next come her three full-grown children, whose grotesque unsavoriness indicates how disreputable the whole stock is. Because one son is too stupid to keep himself alive, his brother and his sister sustain him with what they earn by killing lice. As their mother summons the trio forward, to stand by Reinaert in symbolic fashion, the author terms them "ugly as Barlebaen" (a devil). The remainder of the family is levied and marches up in imposing numbers behind Grimbaert, any reservation about the fox being weaker than respect for Rukenau. Capitalizing on the authority which that demonstration gives her, she concludes her intercession for Reinaert by instructing the king to let the fox be heard, though Nobel must infer that anything less than the utmost leniency in judging Reinaert will be risky.

Thus it seems fair to state that Rukenau has put acquittal in the Cuwaert affair within her nephew's grasp before he has so much as lifted a finger in his own behalf. Since he cannot be proved guilty, in spite of the late Belijn's testimony, his fate depends entirely on Nobel's disposition. Rukenau, whom the queen and Firapeel endorse, has so changed the king that he no longer speaks of Cuwaert's head as Reinaert's insult and now refers to the murder of the hare as a crime which "people say" the fox committed (line 5245). He promises to release Reinaert for the family's sake, moreover, if the fox has an alibi. Reinaert's defense of himself has been reduced to scarcely more than a formality, thanks to Rukenau.

Well aware of what his aunt has accomplished, the fox is finally ready to see out of his own eyes, as he says. He feigns shock and grief that Cuwaert is dead (in effect providing a reason for his prior speechlessness), and he anxiously inquires about Belijn, for he claims to have entrusted both the ram and the hare with three choice objets d'art from his father's treasure, as presents for the king and queen. Rukenau plays along by directing him to describe those valuables, so he does—as the first and most extensive part of a harangue that lasts no fewer than 865 lines. Such long-windedness results from his need to finish talking Nobel into a completely positive frame of mind.

There was a golden ring, he fibs, beset with a three-colored jewel and enameled inside with three Hebrew words which warded off various dangers, according to a learned Jew. The gem had a red section that glowed in the dark, a clear section that cured all bodily ills, and a green section speckled with purple that guarded the wearer against his enemies and made them friends, provided he was noble. Since the king manifestly is, Reinaert flatters, and must be protected, the ring was most fitting for him.

The other two gifts, a comb and a mirror, were allegedly meant for the queen. Reinaert declares that the comb was cut from the thin but indestructible and ivory-white shoulder blade of a still living panther, so that it kept the sweet, hygienic aroma which those animals were reputed by medieval bestiaries to exude. The comb is supposed to have been decorated with many pictures, one of which showed the legendary judgment of Paris. The fox describes that in great detail, perhaps because its theme is bribery and he is once more attempting the same sort of thing himself. He knows from his first trial how easily Nobel is tempted by the prospect of material gain.

In the mirror one could see reflected whatever occurred up to a mile away, and looking at one's own face in it would heal eye ailments, Reinaert contends. He says the frame was of shittim wood, as durable as ebony. He is reminded of how Prince Cleomades in an episode from a thirteenth-century French romance[18] tested an ebony, mechanical horse. Cleomades hurtled many miles through the air, at great peril, before discovering how to control the contraption. Even though this story is utterly tangential, Reinaert devotes thirty-three lines to it, his motive probably being that the prince's predicament strikes him as analogous to his own, when he was accused of Cuwaert's death. With his life at stake, he was for a while unsure of how to manipulate the king but now is sailing along smoothly. Coming back to his imagined mirror, he affirms that its frame was decorated, like the comb, with pictures representing stories. In this case, however, Reinaert does not content himself with just one sample but rather tells four of the tales, all of which are fables intended by him as parables about his enemies.

The first (borrowed from the thirteenth-century Dutch collection *Esopet*)[19] relates how a horse who was envious of a buck had a shepherd ride him for the purpose of shooting the more fleet-footed runner. When the stag still escaped, the man refused to dismount, making the horse the victim of his own malice—something Isegrijn became as a result of the first trial and will become again in Part Four of the sequel. The second fable is fairly similar and also taken from *Esopet*.[20] In it a donkey envies his master's dog for being treated better in spite of doing less, so he tries to behave like his favored rival, affectionately jumping on the terrified man, who has him beaten for his folly. The moral which Reinaert draws is that asses should not be elevated to important positions. Like Rukenau he laments that such ilk are nevertheless on the rise.

Egotism becomes the theme of the third fable, which is not in *Esopet* but was available in other collections, beginning with Marie de France's *Esope*.[21] Because the animals involved in Reinaert's version are specifically Tibeert and Reinaert's own father, the mirror must be thought of as a late addition to the putative treasure. The cat and the elder fox were hunting, we are told, after having sworn to stick together and to share their catch, when they were pursued by dogs. Tibeert climbed a tree, forsaking his partner, who was nearly torn to pieces. How many creatures these days likewise ignore promises for personal advantage, cries Reinaert, hoping to discredit his adversaries by portraying them as the opposite of his own munificent and altruistic self.

The fourth and last fable attributed to the mirror's frame serves that same end. In it (as again in *Esopet*)[22] a wolf choking on a bone is rescued by a crane, only to reward the Good Samaritan by not killing him. Such an ingrate is Isegrijn, Reinaert implies, and he completes his account of the three presents by repeating his and Rukenau's warnings against letting his opponents, branded as rascals, gain power. Before moving on to the second part of his declamation, he reverts to the question of Cuwaert's death by proclaiming an intention to learn eventually who the murderer of his "truest friend" is. With delicious understatement he speculates that even someone at court could know about the crime.

The elaborateness of his description of the nonexistent gifts is meant to make them seem so real that Nobel will believe in his vaunted magnanimity and become more favorably disposed. Surely Reinaert also hopes that the king will concede at least the possibility of his not having lied, after all, when he told of the treasure and conspiracy at his first trial. He is greatly assisted by the silence of Bruun and Isegrijn, who could repeat the wolf's earlier denial that either the hoard or the plot ever existed.

In the first part of Chaucer's "Squire's Tale" the Tartar chief Cambinskan is celebrating his birthday when an ambassador from "the king of Arabie and of Inde" brings four presents. One is a brazen steed which flies, and another is a sword which can cut the thickest armor, inflicting wounds that only a tap with the flat of its blade will heal. The other two gifts are intended for Cambinskan's daughter Canacee. The first is a mirror revealing any threat to ruler or realm, as well as infidelity by any man a woman loves, while the second is a ring which endows its wearer with the mastery of avian language and herbal remedies. Despite the differences both great and small between those curios and Reinaert's, it seems permissible to wonder whether the fox's *Historie* should not be numbered among possible sources for "The Squire's Tale," particularly because of the conjectured allusion to our epic uttered by Simkin in "The Reeve's Tale."[23]

The second section of Reinaert's speech, 234 lines in length, argues that by being angry Nobel is ungrateful, since the fox and his father have each been well deserved of the crown, in stark contrast to Isegrijn. Like Rukenau before him, Reinaert gives an example of his benefactions, but he leads up to it by informing the lion of how his sire restored Nobel's to health long ago. The author of the *Historie* must have been thinking again of *Branche* VI, where Renart, also grieving that his services are unappreciated, cites a cure he performed. Instead of demanding a wolf's hide, Reinaert's father prescribed a seven-year-old wolf's liver. Resembling Ysengrimus, Isegrijn objected that he had not yet reached the age of five.[24] His renitence enables Reinaert, who would generously sacrifice a hundred wolves for the lion's welfare, to portray him once more as selfish and to reiterate the earlier claim that rogues are ousting sages at court. The fox also uses this opportunity to reinforce his conspiracy lie from the first trial by feigning regret that his father became a traitor some time after the cure. He accounts for the professed change by contending that Reinaert Senior was growing senile[25] and was influenced by bad company—presumably Bruun and Isegrijn—although originally the older fox was said to have instigated the plot against Nobel. Again none of the alleged intriguers objects that both the cabal and the treasure are humbug.

Reinaert's example of how he has been a boon to Nobel is a variant of Nivardus's lion's-share episode, though it probably comes to the *Historie* via some later version, such as *Branche* XVI of the *Roman de Renart*.[26] It makes explicit an illogicality implicit in *Branche* I and *Proto-Reinaert*—the fact that the fox's judge is also carnivorous. Nobel was delighted with Reinaert's division of prey, in contrast to Isegrijn's, as the fox reminds him, warning yet another time against letting the wolf have power. Reinaert concludes this second part of his 865-line tour de force by bluntly stressing that his merits are being poorly repaid.

In the third section, consisting of only ten lines, he revives the counselor theme from Rukenau's address by asserting that he has distinguished himself through his good judgment, which has made him essential at court. He ends the whole verbal marathon with a promise that he will welcome punishment if any crime is proved against him.

Nobel's change of heart is sufficiently complete for the king to exonerate Reinaert from the charge of having killed Cuwaert and besmirched the crown, in effect admitting that guilt cannot be pinned on anyone. Despite not saying so, he has to realize that the fox is too important to be sacrificed, moreover. Reinaert's clan must be respected, and his cleverness is often needed. The sheer length of his speech has surely been advantageous in itself, by forcing the lion to consider fully the consequences of an execution. It seems also to have made Nobel forget that the treasure at Kriekeput belongs to him now, if those riches do exist. Instead of demanding them, he and the queen merely beg Reinaert to look for the ring, comb, and mirror. Of course, should an expedition to Hulsterloo be waged, the fox can cover his tracks by declaring that the cache has again been spirited away. His fearsome family insures his impunity, for which reason he can end Part Two of the sequel with a jest, even though it began with an earnest threat against his life. He promises Nobel that he will indeed search for the gifts, if the king provides whatever help he needs.

Part Three: Verses 6244–6778. Before Reinaert came to court the second time, Isegrijn alluded vaguely to offenses which would cost the fox his life. Now that Reinaert is about to go free, the wolf plays his trump by detailing two of those wrongs, while his wife Eerswinde adds a third. Like Ysengrin in *Branche* VI, Isegrijn wants revenge above all for the she-wolf's rape—that primordial complaint which triggered litigation in *Van den Vos Reynaerde, Branche* I, and Pierre de Saint-Cloud's romance, as well as in the *Historie.* The assault which Isegrijn describes did not take place in the entrance to Malpertuus, however, but rather in a situation similar to the fishing episodes of *Ysengrimus* and *Branche* III. He indignantly reports that the fox sent Eerswinde into a wintry morass to fish with her tail. When it was frozen fast, Reinaert somehow raped her. Much as in *Branche* II-Va, when Renart has Hersent in a more convenient posture and her mate catches up with them, Isegrijn discovered the strugglers in the sump, frightening the fox away. In order to be liberated, Eerswinde had to forgo the end of her tail. Her yelps attracted armed villagers (more reminiscent of the ones who attack Bruun at Lamfroyt's house in *Proto-Reinaert* than those in *Branche* I), and they nearly killed both her and Isegrijn.

Reinaert defends himself, as in *Branches* II-Va and VI, by alleging that he only wanted to help Eerswinde. Had she been less greedy, he says in a rejoinder akin to Renart's comment on the fishing incidents discussed in *Branche* VI, she would not have been trapped. Being chased by the peasants was good for the wolves, he maintains, because it warmed their blood. Solemnly he swears to Nobel that he would never lie. Eerswinde, who is

present at court, unlike Hersent in *Branche* VI, does not corroborate her husband's testimony, even though she shares his ire.

Instead, she chides the fox for tricking her in a less serious
affair on another occasion. Copying Renart with Ysengrin in
Branche IV, he escaped from a well by luring her into it, but this
exploitation was so insignificant that he departs from his usual
practice by admitting it. It should serve as a lesson to Eerswinde,
he lectures, teaching her to be more cautious. Just as the well
and pond incidents are linked together in *Branche* VI, provoking
a little sermon by Renart, so (in different order) one follows the
other in the *Historie* and occasions some further vulpine moralizing.

Isegrijn's second complaint about Reinaert is even less dam-
aging than Eerswinde's lament about the well. In fact, it discredits the wolf rather than the fox. Since Reinaert's accusers have
achieved no success by first narrating their versions of what he
did to them, Isegrijn reverses that procedure with this last charge
to be brought. He lets the fox tell the court what happened when
the two of them found a mysterious cave one day (an adventure
perhaps inspired by another fable in *Esopet*).[27] In spite of being
famished, the wolf would not venture in until Reinaert had ex-
plored the hole. In its depths the fox met a fierce female ape with
three ugly young. Both they and the room were so befouled that
he could hardly breathe. To keep from being killed, he pretended
that the slut was his aunt, and he complimented her on having
handsome children. His courtesy won him his fill of various meats
and a sample to carry with him when he left. This he presented
to the wolf as a token of what could be obtained through
diplomacy.

Although warned against forthrightness with the apes, Isegrijn
marched into their den and swore that the three repulsive brats
should be drowned. Feeding them was a waste, he spat, as he
stormed toward the pantry. Instead of being treated hospitably,
like dishonest Reinaert, he was nearly shredded on account of his
candid boorishness. Some lies are proper, as the fox told Grimbaert on the way to court in Part One of the continuation. The
author of the *Historie* evidently wanted to stress that his condem-

nation of Reinaert's mendacity does not extend to the cosmetic retouching of truth occasionally required by politeness.

Like the wolf in *Branche* VI, Isegrijn is forced to demand a duel, which the fox suggested earlier, if he is to obtain satisfaction for the suffering he feels his foe has caused him, even though his laceration by the apes resulted from his own intractable stupidity. He specifies two crimes which cry for retribution, whatever the risk. They are his supposed participation in the plot against Nobel and the rape of Eerswinde. Reinaert is more reluctant to take up the wolf's gage than Renart is in *Branche* VI, perhaps because no weapons will be sanctioned apart from tooth and nail, but he is consoled by the fact that Isegrijn's forepaws, which were flayed at the end of the first trial, have not yet healed. His bigger opponent will be about as handicapped as Ysengrin becomes in *Branche* VI, when the latter's left arm is broken. Reinaert accepts the challenge, and Part Three concludes as Tibeert and Bruun become Isegrijn's guarantors, with Grimbaert and one of Rukenau's sons seconding the fox. Instead of being delayed for two weeks, like the contest in *Branche* VI, this duel will be held the following morning, on the third and final day of action in the sequel, which therefore spans the same amount of time as *Van den Vos Reynaerde*.

Part Four: Verses 6779–7794. During the night before the fight, Rukenau prepares Reinaert, making recommendations partly inspired by *Branche* VI. She has his body shaved and greased, rendering him physically as elusive as he has figuratively been, but his tail remains bushy, for he is to soak it with his urine in the course of the bout and to slap Isegrijn in the face with it.[28] Rukenau terminates her training session by insuring the fox's victory with a magic formula in incomprehensible mumbo jumbo, the idea for which the *Historie*'s author also took from *Branche* VI, where Renart would like to protect himself with a charm. Trusting in the efficacy of those "holy words," Reinaert sleeps until the sun is high, when his uncle the otter brings him a duck for breakfast. His relatives contribute more than the fox's family prior to *Branche* VI's battle because Renart is a private individual, not a political leader.

After stepping into a ring marked out on bare ground, each contender utters a sacred oath, as in *Branche* VI, but the relics are borne by the two umpires of the duel, Firapeel and the lynx, rather than by a priest. Perhaps Belijn was the only ecclesiastic among the whole assemblage. Isegrijn swears that Reinaert is a murderer and a deceiver, while the fox formally commits perjury with his vow that the wolf is lying.

When the fight begins, he obeys his aunt's instructions from the previous night, blinding Isegrijn with urine and dust and evading lunges with slippery quickness. The wolf knocks him down twice, however, and jumps on him the second time. Reinaert almost escapes by scratching out one of Isegrijn's eyes, but the wolf bites his hand, as Ysengrin bites Renart's finger in *Branche* VI. Rather than surrender, Reinaert distracts Isegrijn by promising to serve him in exchange for release, like Renart prior to the duel in *Branche* VI. Reminding us of *Ysengrimus,* action is suspended for protracted conversation here. Despite his pain, the fox is in no hurry, and the wolf rejects his deal with comparable verbosity, even though Isegrijn's jaws are locked on Reinaert's paw.

In keeping with *Branche* VI and the medieval presuppositions of judicial combat, the wolf should proceed to win,[29] but justice no longer prevailed in the world as viewed by the *Historie*'s author. Cunning could triumph and often did, he wanted his readers to know. Reinaert succeeds regardless of perjury, rape, murder, and whatever other sins can be ascribed to him. He does so, moreover, with an underhandedness that symbolizes his customary treachery, for he grabs Isegrijn's testicles.[30] The wolf screams and faints, releasing Reinaert's paw, whereupon the fox drags him arrogantly around the ring, still holding him by his scrotum, and kicks him in contempt.

Led by trumpeting minstrels, Reinaert and a throng of well-wishers parade to the throne, where Nobel pronounces him cleared of the charges made by Isegrijn. The lion fails to realize that the fox's victory confirms the story of a conspiracy, so that logically the wolf, the bear, and the badger should all be punished for treason. Having forgotten about the plot as well as about his ownership of the treasure, Nobel intends to reconcile Isegrijn with Reinaert as soon as the wolf has recovered.

The fox discredits everyone who was slow to side with him, comparing such opportunists to a pack of hungry dogs which admire a fellow hound for snatching a bone from their master's kitchen, until they discover that the cook scalded the thief's rear with boiling water. Since in this analogy the bone stealer corresponds to Isegrijn, Reinaert is also able to brand the wolf as selfish. How many knavish dogs, he exclaims, are to be found at court with a bone in their mouth, having betrayed the commonweal for their own advantage. Of course those words are most applicable to him, but he hastens to assert that he and his family are beyond reproach. He caps this last of his lengthy speeches (121 lines) with a saccharine declaration of his undying love for the king. Whereas Nobel was suspicious of flattery at the beginning of both trials, he delights in it now.

He has been won over by Reinaert and Rukenau to such an extent that he names the fox his deputy and affirms that he intends to operate entirely on Reinaert's advice, though by admonishing the fox three times to be virtuous (lines 7570, 7573, and 7578) he hints that Reinaert still lacks his total confidence.[31] Even so, he says that the court cannot dispense with the fox. Thus he avows what Reinaert and Rukenau have known all along and counted on as a crucial factor. Henceforth the animal kingdom will be ruled consistently by that combination which Machiavelli later recommended to every prince—the power of the lion and the fox's craftiness.

Reinaert's clan thank the king for the honor bestowed on their chief, and Rukenau guarantees that her nephew will remain loyal, while he kneels to express his own gratitude and promise of devotion. Meanwhile, wretched Iegrijn has been carried from the ring and revived by physicians, who are sure of his recuperation. Though the author does not say so, perhaps he nonetheless meant for the loss of an eye to symbolize Isegrijn's stupidity, since the wolf has never been able to see the world quite as it really is, having been partially blinded by a fatal insistence on viewing it the way he wants it to be. With the court adjourning, Reinaert takes leave from the king and queen.

Before trailing him home, the author interjects a sixty-eight-line comment, letting us know how we should interpret the *Historie,* as we noted at the outset of this chapter. Cynical but articulate hypocrites like the fox have taken charge everywhere, in both Church and state, we are told, and whoever lacks his amoral glibness has no future. Justice, loyalty, and truth have been replaced by greed, cunning, hatred, and arrogance. Money is all that matters at court, and even women have been tainted by it. No help can be expected from the clergy, which is also decadent.

The author, who was about as pessimistic as Nivardus and shared the general gloominess of the Late Middle Ages, felt that unscrupulous politicians were gaining control because society on the whole was rotten. Those men were a gauge of everyone's corruption. Certainly Reinaert can only succeed with Nobel's permission, and we know how morally weak the lion has been ever since Arnout had him condemn the fox. When a ruler lacks virtue, his court is not likely to preserve it either. Perhaps Firapeel does, but the leopard is too naive and modest to defend morality well. How sad that Reinaert's principal opponent is Isegrijn the wolf!

The fox travels to Malpertuus in the company of over forty relatives, whom he plans to further with his new influence, just as he will also hinder his enemies. The privilege of persecuting his kind, granted to the bear and the wolf in the denouement of *Van den Vos Reynaerde,* has tacitly been abrogated, and the fox is now in a position to make life miserable for Bruun and Isegrijn. After thanking his kin and parting from them, he informs Hermeline of all that has happened. In a thirty-five-line epilogue the author contends that his story should be believed for its ethical and educational value, and he confesses that he would be happy for it to remain unchanged, although improvements would have his blessing.

Reinaerts Historie is neither so bad as has been held traditionally nor quite so good as Heeroma has asserted,[32] for he ignored its definite, if by and large minor, flaws in his revisionist enthusiasm. One must consider that the great amount of prolix cant in the poem is meant to be distasteful, since it is the main tool of political swindlers. That the fox has much more assistance here than in Willem's continuation to *Proto-Reinaert,* depending to a large extent on the strength of his clan, conforms to the reality of politics. If a long-winded shyster is less engaging than Willem's virtuoso of psychological finesse, we must remember the cautionary purpose of the *Historie.* Its fox may be someone with whom we do not identify so readily—or even at all—yet surely he is still too common a figure, in the twentieth century no less than in the fourteenth. The work is bleak and slow-paced, though perhaps less wearisome than many critics have thought, when understood. It can clearly be improved, and we will see that it was in the Low-German remake entitled *Reynke de Vos,* but also in its original form it warrants respect as a major contribution to late medieval literature.

Proto-Reinaert, Van den Vos Reynaerde, and *Reinaerts Historie* form a series that could be labeled the Rogue's Progress, since in the course of those three epics Reinaert rises from the gallows to exile and then, if not to the throne itself, at least to the royal footstool. Conversely, society declines, from dignity and victory to contemptibility and stalemate, then on to ignominiousness and defeat. Maybe because the fox could hardly climb higher or the state sink lower, no fifteenth-century author continued the process of casting Reinaert in a new relationship to his fellow beasts by extending old material, though the *Historie* was altered several times before 1500. Our final chapter deals with the ways in which its format and import were changed in early printings.

Chapter Five

The Incunabular Fox

While *Reinaerts Historie* was issued from more than a single press in the final quarter of the fifteenth century, the *editio princeps* of *Van den Vos Reynaerde* was not undertaken till 1812. Late medieval publishers must have felt that readers would generally prefer the longer, more complete work, or perhaps *Van den Vos Reynaerde* had already slipped into oblivion. Balduinus's Latin translation of it had not, however. *Reynardus Vulpes* was brought out in 1473 or 1474, preceding the *Historie* into print and becoming one of the first animal epics to be published, if not the very first.

Reynardus Vulpes

It was issued at Utrecht by Nicolaes Ketelaer and Geraerd de Leempt, who took no care with it, permitting many errors, as if they thought it unimportant. They probably printed it from a manuscript belonging to a monastery in Utrecht and meant it to be amusement for the clergy in idle moments, particularly since Balduinus had inserted moralizing comments every so often. Ketelaer and de Leempt may have had no interest in· *Van den Vos Reynaerde,* even if it was available to them.[1]

They are likely to have been responsible for dividing *Reynardus Vulpes* into nine chapters with prose headings, and they definitely appended an epilogue,[2] which consists of two distichs, suggesting how the poem should be interpreted. In the first couplet we are told that the fox stands for all wicked deceivers, whom rulers, represented by the exalted lion, detest. The last two lines declare that the fox's spirit *(vis)* dominates civilian, military, and ecclesiastic life, though he himself is outlawed. Society is plagued with trickery, in other words, as practiced by Reynardus. No more than Willem's king, however, is Balduinus's consistently the fox's enemy. (In his intercalated comments Balduinus shows that he, too, viewed Reynardus as an evil sharper.)

William Caxton's Source

The first edition of *Reinaerts Historie* is not in verse. It is a revision in prose, which Gheraert Leeu negligently printed in 1479 at Gouda and which Jacob Jacobszoon van der Meer brought out again at Delft in 1485. Leeu must have thought that average readers would prefer a prose text, and in general during the later fifteenth century verse was less popular. Like *Reynardus Vulpes,* this variant of the *Historie* is divided into sections with descriptive headings (forty-six chapters in all). As also in the Latin translation, a new prologue replaces Arnout's and Willem's, which was essentially kept in the original *Historie.* Whereas Balduinus's is merely a dedication to his patron, however, the Gouda prologue instructs us to read what follows much as the epilogue to *Reynardus Vulpes* would have us understand the Latin poem. Reinaert, that is to say, is every swindler once again, operating everywhere. Even though the *Historie* has not been changed significantly, it is now supposed to be an exposé of the subtle wiles which take their toll among all three social classes (nobility, both secular and ecclesiastic, merchants, and commoners), so that readers from every walk of life will guard against being duped. Apparently the unknown author of the prose rendering felt that the *Historie*'s actual focus on slippery politicos is too narrow.

A version of that prose rendering (probably in manuscript) is what William Caxton translated into English as *Reynart the Foxe* and first released at Westminster in 1481. Because his text is more correct in some places than Leeu's, he must have worked from a better copy than the one which Leeu printed, no matter that the dates involved suggest a dependence on Leeu. He kept the same prologue, not reinterpreting the *Historie* at all.[3]

The Missing Link and *Reynke de Vos*

Around 1487 Leeu, who had moved from Gouda to Antwerp in 1484, published a form of the original *Historie* in verse, which has survived only in a few small fragments, now in the Cambridge University Library.[4] These fragments (containing parts of Reinaert's first confession to the badger, their arrival at court, and the fox's condemnation) show that the 1487 edition was broken into chapters, like the prose *Historie,* although with more divisions, and that each chapter had a descriptive title. In addition, moralizing commentaries preceded some chapters, and many woodcuts illustrated the story. Leeu had evidently grown curious to see whether a nicer format for the *Historie*—aimed at upper-class readers—would not return a prettier profit than the plebeian prose rendition.

Further information about his 1487 poem, which we will term the Missing Link, can be gleaned from *Reynke de Vos,* which was printed by the so-called "Poppy Press" at Lübeck in 1498. This Low-German revision of the *Historie* is based on the vanished work because it incorporates the prose commentary and a number of errors from the Cambridge Fragments.[5] It consists of two prologues in prose, replacing Willem's and Arnout's introduction to *Van den Vos Reynaerde,* a text of 3,422 couplets divided into four books, which are in turn subdivided into chapters with descriptive headings in prose, and prose commentaries every so often. Like the Missing Link it was embellished with woodcuts to increase its appeal,[6] and to facilitate comprehension the various points in its prologues and glosses are numbered.

Since the second preface and some commentaries have rough counterparts in a Dutch chapbook, *Reynaert de Vos,* published at Antwerp in 1564, we can assume that they derive from the Missing Link, which must be a common parent of both later offspring. The text of the chapbook was basically supplied by some version of the prose *Historie,* however, so it offers little help in judging to what extent *Reynke*'s verses reproduce the Missing Link. A comparison of the Cambridge Fragments with the corresponding sections of *Reynke* indicates that the anonymous Low-German editor, who is likely to have been a Franciscan monk,[7] translated rather freely, not even holding to the same chapter divisions. The part of *Reynke* which is most enlightening about the Missing Link is the first prologue, which reads as if it were lifted virtually intact from that source.[8]

It begins by stating that before the birth of Christ there were wise men called poets, some of whom cast their wisdom in the form of fables, for the sake of easy remembrance. One of these animal stories from antiquity is *Reinaerts Historie,* the author of the prologue mistakenly contends, and he goes on to identify himself as Hinrec van Alcmaer, a teacher in the employ of the Duke of Lorraine, at whose request he purports to have translated the *Historie* from Italian and French. His astonishing abuse of poetic license was no doubt inspired by Willem's prologue to *Van den Vos Reynaerde,* though with the intention of making the *Historie* more prestigious. (One wonders how readers who knew it in prose reacted to that extravagance.) In conclusion the prologue's author also claims credit for separating the original work into four parts and adding explanations of its meaning.

If *Reynke*'s first prologue was indeed composed for the Missing Link, as is universally assumed, that earlier work was likewise split into four books. We gain a name we can attach to it, moreover, unless Hinrec is as fictional as the assertion that his "translation" was made from Italian and French. A lawyer with the same name is known to have lived in Utrecht before being expelled in 1477, but we have no way of ascertaining whether the two men are identical.[9] A further difficulty is that Hinrec could also have been lying about a benefactor, to plume himself with borrowed feathers. The uncertain duke's alleged interest in Reinaert could be another touch copied from the prologue by Willem and Arnout.

Instead of distinguishing his own work from Hinrec's in any way, the editor of *Reynke* presented it as if its immediate author were Hinrec. Not only did he transfer his first preface from the Missing Link. In the preface he also had Hinrec maintain that "this present book" (*dyt yeghenwerdyge boek*) was translated from Italian and French into German (*in dudesche sprake*), while Hinrec actually rendered the *Historie* into Dutch, provided he was the Missing Link's author, of course. Perhaps whatever could be sold as a foreigner's authentic craft had better prospects in Lübeck than anything known to be a local reproduction.

Reynke's second prologue attempts primarily to show how the Low-German poem is a picture of society. It contains representatives from all four social strata, we are told, beginning with workers like the horse, the mule, the donkey, and the ox. They constitute the basic class, from which the others sprang. The second estate, in ascending order, is called that of the merchants, who resemble hoarding animals. The third class, which is said to be supported by the first two, comprises the clergy, although they are compared not to the ram but rather to the badger, that snickering fake who plays at being father confessor. Of churchmen, we read, little is expressed in *Reynke,* except that they are obliquely criticized for greed and unchasteness. The fourth estate, also living off the first two, is made up both of lords "who consider themselves noble" but are rapacious like wolves, bears, lynxes, and leopards, the editor declares with evident distaste, and of less eminent worthies such as the fox, the monkey, or the dog. Their retainers purportedly correspond to "little biting animals," even though no servants appear in the epic. [10]

All society is governed by a monarch, for the maintenance of peace and justice, the second prologue continues, and the king of the beasts is the lion, who tries criminals but not always in proper fashion. In the editor's opinion *Reynke* proves that courtiers seeking to enrich themselves will be thwarted and that wise counselors are better than avaricious ones, for no land can be ruled well without good judgment. "Thus this book is about a prince and his court," we are informed, but "it is also about the condition of simple commoners and about liars and deceivers" like the fox. In conclusion thirty-one of the thirty-six animals and birds named in the Low-German poem are cited.

To determine what elements of *Reynke*'s second prologue were borrowed from an equivalent introductory passage in the Missing Link, we must compare it with the preface to the 1564 chapbook, [11] for it is less likely than *Reynke*'s first prologue to have been appropriated almost entirely from Hinrec. After an exhortation to read carefully for edification, the chapbook's preface states that a royal court will be presented first; the lot of common folk, second; third, the nature of deceivers; and last, the triumph of wisdom, which rulers should seek in their counselors, as opposed to avarice. We are then apprised that clergy, to be criticized obliquely for greed and unchasteness, will be represented by the badger; high nobility by wolves, bears, lynxes, and leopards; lower nobility by such as the fox, the monkey, the dog, and the cat; and workers by horses, oxen, and donkeys, for example. A short final section, without any list of names, declares that the story to follow combines both pleasure and profit.

Reynke's second prologue clearly contains much of the same material, offered in more or less reverse order. We can deduce that Hinrec, who was surely prompted by the preface to the prose *Historie,* included the concept of a microcosm mirroring social classes, the rather contradictory view of Reinaert as both a swindler and a wise adviser, the implication that Isegrijn stands for self-serving courtiers, the mistaking of appearance for reality in construing Grimbaert as a priest, even though he is married (for he still has a wife in *Reynke*), and the comment that churchmen are chided in the *Historie* for carnality and materialism. Merchants and servants are likely to have been omitted, since they are not mentioned in the preface to the chapbook, where Nobel's role and conduct as judge are also ignored.

Hinrec's misconception of the badger may have resulted from negligence, while his twisted, or perhaps cynical, idea of the fox as a good counselor could reflect a concern to make the *Historie* as interesting as possible to men in power. As Heeroma has affirmed, agreement between the chapbook's prologue and *Reynke*'s second one implies that Hinrec separated the *Historie* into four books according to the notion that the first portrays a royal court; the second, commoners; the third, liars; and the fourth, wisdom's superiority. [12] We will find that the introductions to Books II, III, and IV of *Reynke,* which in all likelihood conform to Hinrec's divisions, echo that same rationale.

The Low-German editor's commencement with the base of the social pyramid, his snide remark about predatory lords styling themselves as inherently superior, and his forthright recognition

that the upper classes are sustained by the lower ones all suggest
that he identified with the average citizens of Lübeck, though
he probably wrote for the city's patricians. [13] One finds this sympathy confirmed in *Reynke*'s commentaries, along with the concern
for justice and morality which is also expressed in the second
prologue. For example, in the fifth and sixth points of the gloss
to Chapter 7 in Book Two (abbreviated to II,7.5–6) powerful
courtiers like the wolf and the bear are accused of battening on
"the sour work, the sweat and blood of inferiors," and poor
offenders are said to be prosecuted to the full extent of the law
while rich ones are excused.

   Despite assuring us, at the end of his poem, that we may skip
his scholia, the Low-German editor devoted a great deal of space
to them and would have been disappointed at any reader interested
in the fox's vicissitudes only for the sake of entertainment. His
glosses normally follow, rather than precede, the chapter or group
of chapters with which they deal, in contrast to Hinrec's (as
indicated by the Cambridge Fragments). While they tend to give
advice based on events in *Reynke* proper or to comment on related
aspects of life, the purpose of some annotations is to elucidate
the epic rather than to admonish or to educate us. In IV,2.4, for
instance, we are presented with a reason for why the female wolf,
now called Ghyremod, does not corroborate her husband's charge
that she was raped. She changes the subject, directing everyone's
attention to a less embarrassing incident, because a compromised
woman should guard her honor with all her wiles.

   The most important explanatory remark is IV,10.2, in which
the editor tells us how Reynke should be viewed. No longer first
and foremost a crooked politician or even a swindler, the fox has
become something still more fundamental. Together with his
clan he stands for "all those who are wise only in mundane
things." He is the totally secularized and amoral atheist of the
period around 1500 that we associate with Renaissance Italy (à
la Cesare Borgia) rather than with late medieval Germany, but
that type must have stalked the streets of Lübeck as well as of
Rome.

A comparison of the Low-German editor's commentaries with the ones in the 1564 chapbook indicates that at least twenty derive from Hinrec's glosses in the Missing Link. [14] Those twenty or so suggest that Hinrec dealt in his notes almost exclusively with practical tips, for life either in general or at court. He and Leeu appear to have felt that lessons on conduct, particularly for aristocrats, would help their publication sell best.

The body of *Reynke* contains numerous departures from the *Historie,* and it is impossible to judge with certainty how many are due to Hinrec versus the Lübeck editor. Nearly without exception, in any case, those modifications constitute improvements. An analysis, or even a list, of them all would be tedious and unnecessary for our purposes, so we will limit ourselves to the more important ones, proceeding book by book. [15]

Book One. Verses 169–98: In the course of Grymbart the badger's reply to Ysegrym the wolf's initial accusations, as the court is being informed of Ysegrym's sins against Reynke, the original account (lasting nine lines) of how the wolf ate up all the fish which the fox threw from a wagon is tripled in length. Before Grymbart deals with the manner in which Ysegrym cheated Reynke on this occasion, he relates how his uncle got aboard the cart, thus making a complete little story of the incident which had previously been truncated. Reynke sprawled in the middle of the road as if dead, not flinching even when the wagoner drew a sword to skin him. Instead of being flayed on the spot, however, he was flung atop the fish. Clearly apparent here is influence from *Branche* XIV of the *Roman de Renart,* in which Primaut is threatened with a sword, while *Branche* III could also be reflected. Did the Lübeck editor read French and have access to a manuscript of the *Roman de Renart?* That Hinrec did appears more probable, but we can only guess.

Verses 199–220: The badger's second example of how his uncle has been mistreated by the wolf is also expanded, either Hinrec or the Low-German editor being again more detailed than Arnout and the *Historie*'s author about the fox's pains on behalf of an ingrate. Grymbart is therefore likelier to elicit sympathy for Reynke than Grimbaert arouses for Reinaert. Whereas Grimbaert does not explain how Isegrijn obtained the ham he totally consumed, Grymbart relates that Reynke slipped through the window of a smokehouse in order to provide Ysegrym with a slaughtered pig, which the wolf devoured while the fox was under attack by dogs. The seduction of the peasant in *Ysengrimus* and *Branche* V, of which Arnout was probably thinking, has been replaced, and Arnout's curious addition about the fox being thrown into a sack (lines 230–35 of the *Historie*) has been deleted.

Verses 457–878: Brun the bear's quest for honey takes place at night rather than during the afternoon. In line 588 of the *Historie* Reinaert excuses his delay in greeting Bruun upon the latter's arrival at Malpertuus by alleging that he has been reading vespers, but it is still early enough in the day for the fox to be hot after eating the hen and for court to be in session when the bear comes rolling in. Either Hinrec or the Lübeck editor must have thought that a time more in keeping with vespers would be more appropriate for a bear and a fox to go prowling, since they would prefer the cover of darkness. (In *Branche* II-Va Brun says that he and Renart were supposed to wait for nightfall before raiding Constant des Noes's pantry for honey.) In daylight's greater visibility the bear is also less likely to stick his entire head into a split log. When Reynke and Brun arrive at their destination, the carpenter, named Rustevyl, is already in bed. Aroused by Brun's roars, Rustevyl summons his fellow peasants from a party, and they must run home to fetch their weapons.

There are three slight additions and a couple of minor changes within the episode which are worth mentioning since they show how meticulous the editor (or editors) could be. (1) Not only does Reynke claim to have dined on honey because he is poor, but in lines 555–56 he provides a better reason, too. He insinuates that he needs fresh honey for his potency, and, indeed, medieval lovers seem to have found it an aphrodisiac.[16] (2) We are told in line 617 that the wedges holding the log open are very slick, so we might more readily believe that the fox could pull them out. (3) In lines 760–61 the priest promises not just the pardoning of sins for the rescue of his "maid," Yutte, but pardon plus two barrels of beer, which should be a greater inducement, particularly since his parishioners seem to carouse.[17] (4) Reynke no longer thinks of the bear as the greatest danger to him at court but only as one of his enemies (line 819). (5) Rather than revolve his painfully battered hulk, Brun inches his way to the palace, taking three days to make what remains of the trip (lines 877–78).

Verses 1090–1166: Probably Hinrec, rather than the more religious Lübeck editor, inserted a raping of Ghyremod into the episode with Tibeert's replacement, Hyntze the cat, at the point where he has just been snared in Martinet's noose. Reynke departs before the priest's family attacks, like his counterpart in *Branche* I of the *Roman de Renart,* and Reinaert's joke about the one "clapper" is simply dropped, rather than being given to Hyntze, as it is given to Tibert in *Branche* I. Reynke is eager to visit the other woman in his life, aware that her husband is not at home. He is curious to learn what his enemy is telling the court, and he wants to renew his old adultery, which is cited as the main cause of his conflict with Ysegrym. It turns out that Ghyremod is not at home either, but the fox greets her cubs, calling them "my dearest stepchildren." That they are the litter on which he once urinated, according to Ysegrym's early testimony, is doubtful.

Soon, at dawn, their mother returns, asking whether anyone has been to see her, as if she has expected Reynke. The innuendo that her whelps are illegitimate so infuriates her that she rushes away in search of the fox. When she finds him, he runs from her, jumping through a broken wall in which she is caught. Ysegrym does not interrupt Reynke now, and Ghyremod must eventually free herself. Apparently she refrains from telling her mate about her embarrassment, because at the fox's second trial Ysegrym still reports only the rape in the polder. While not sharpening the conflict between Reynke and the wolf, therefore, the new skirmish does help to make it more prominent within the poem as a whole and somewhat less preponderant in Book Four, which is devoted almost entirely to their feud. Again we find influence from the *Roman de Renart*—in this case *Branche* II-Va—and it tends to confirm Hinrec's authorship of the insertion.

Verses 1534–82: An altered detail in the story, from Reynke's first confession to Grymbart, of how he and the wolf went chicken stealing in an attic one night is interesting because it is an improvement definitely made by the Lübeck editor. Part of the equivalent passage from the Cambridge Fragments shows that, by having Reinaert jab Isegrijn, Hinrec essentially followed the original *Historie,* in which the fox pushes the wolf, whereas in *Reynke* the two enter through an open window which the fox lets fall as he slips out, causing the wolf to topple from fright. Thus Reynke does not compromise himself like Reinaert in the various editions of the *Historie.* The Low-German fox is closer to Arnout's, who eggs Isengrijn on until the wolf plunges of his own accord.

Verse 1764: Although Grymbart still has a wife (lines 2185–93), nothing is said of the ram's spouse when Bellyn leads the court in demanding Reynke's death at the fox's initial trial. The contradition brought about between *Proto-Reinaert* and Willem's continuation by Hawi's inclusion in the former work is eliminated, making the ram more acceptable as court chaplain. In the Cambridge Fragments he is accompanied by "Lady Olewij," but she is his aunt, while in the original *Historie* "Madam Olewi" remains Belijn's wife. The Lübeck editor went one step further than Hinrec in correcting Willem's oversight, despite the fact that Hinrec had already gone far enough.

Verses 1851–56: The wolf, the bear, and the cat continue to function as hangmen, yet now at least we are told that Nobel has designated not only Hyntze but also Ysegrym and Brun to execute their common enemy.

Verses 1893–97, 2064–75, and 2609–20: In these lines the worst blunder of the *Historie*'s author is rectified. We noted early in Chapter Four that Tiecelijn the raven still has to apprise Isegrijn, Bruun, and Tibeert of the reversal in Reinaert's fortunes, even though the whole court moves to the gallows in the *Historie*'s account of the first trial. In *Reynke* everyone at that trial again goes over to the gibbet. The fox's foes do not hear him implicate them in his father's alleged conspiracy, however, because the royal couple order him down from the ladder on which he has been making his confession, to tell them privately about the treasure. One of the nicest improvements in the Low-German poem is the complete removal of any messenger who acquaints the wolf, the bear, and the cat with what has transpired. They themselves listen to Nobel announce his change of mind, just as they ought to hear him when he delivers the same speech in the *Historie.* These corrections should be attributed to Hinrec rather than to the Lübeck editor because they occur in the 1564 chapbook, as well as in *Reynke,* but not in the prose *Historie.* The chapbook's author, like *Reynke*'s, must have taken them from the Missing Link.

Verses 2514–17: Unlike Cuwaert in *Van den Vos Reynaerde* and the *Historie,* Lampe the hare no longer claims to have been friends with a dog, since either Hinrec or the Lübeck editor considered such a relationship too unnatural. For the sake of verisimilitude, Rijn, or Ryn, has become Lampe's enemy, and the hare purports to have hidden from him in "Husterlo." Reinaert's wish that the dog were present, to testify also, is cut, because Ryn is indeed present now (line 1770). Even so, the fox does not call upon him.

Verses 3060–70: In the *Historie* as in *Van den Vos Reynaerde* the fox warns Belijn in only a few words not to open the pouch that is supposed to contain letters for the king. Since the ram's obedience must override his curiosity in order for him to be victimized, the editor of *Reynke* (or was it Hinrec?) felt that the fox's injunction needed strengthening. He guaranteed Bellyn's cooperation by having Reynke say that the satchel is tied in a special way, enabling Nobel to ascertain whether it has been tampered with. The expansion here is another fine example of the attention given to psychological detail in the Lübeck epic.

Book One concludes where *Van den Vos Reynaerde* ends, though the vixen Ermelyn has persuaded her husband to stay at home, as in the *Historie.*

Book Two. A short prose introduction announces that the second part of *Reynke,* in which the author especially discusses the condition of men and their faults, begins with a number of birds complaining over the fox as they head for court to join the celebration in honor of Brun and Ysegrym. Seven woodcuts follow, showing various fowl, and each picture is preceded by a

four-verse caption which relates how unhappy the birds portrayed
are with Reynke, who preys on them. All of the captions together
comprise lines 3247–74, which were added by the Lübeck editor.[18] Chapter 1, commencing at line 3275, then picks up the
plot of the *Historie* again.

Verse 3350: The rabbit's remark in lines 3555–56 of the *Historie,* that Scerpenebbe is approaching with her husband (even
though she has been killed), is omitted, removing another
inconsistency.[19]

Verse 3821: The moral, to the effect that the best-educated
people are not always the wisest, which Reinaert drew from
Isegrijn's encounter with the mare in lines 4101–4105 of the
Historie is deleted, probably as being alien to the greediness which
the wolf is supposed to represent in both *Reynke* and the Missing
Link.

Verses 3841–4071: A new, 231-line speech has been substituted for Reinaert's 138-line defense of lying in the *Historie.*
Whereas the idea that the world corrupts is merely an introductory motif there, it becomes the theme of the surrogate harangue.
Rejecting with a profane expletive Grymbart's concern over the
possible consequences of Lampe's head, Reynke avers that sinning
is inevitable, the hare tempted him irresistibly, and both Lampe
and Bellyn were contemptibly stupid. "But let's change the subject," he demands, whereupon he maintains that Nobel and many
prelates—the leaders of Church and state—set bad examples.
The remaining 204 lines of his tirade elaborate on that assertion.

In verses 3973–75, which repeat the substance of gloss I,3.3,
he opines, "It's true that many priests in Lombardy have a mistress, but none do in this country," even though he knows from
recent experience that local divines not only have mistresses but
also beget children by them. This is the least intelligent change
in the whole Low-German poem.

Reynke speaks for whoever composed his screed, because the
first sentence of the introduction to Book Two refers to it with
the words, "the poet talks especially about the condition of men
and their faults." "The poet" therefore identifies with the fox in
this instance. Since the first sentence of Book Two's introduction

probably derives from Hinrec, it must have been he, rather than the Lübeck editor, who decided that Reinaert's original lecture to Grimbaert could be put to better use. The Low-German editor then added some touches of his own, like Reynke's regrettable pronouncement about celibate priests.

Verses 4097–4231: Instead of pretending that he met the ape, now called Marten, before leaving home, Reynke and Grymbart actually do chance upon that official as they approach the court, so that he becomes a definite asset. Much of the conversation which the fox just purports to have had with Mertijn in the *Historie* really does take place in the Low-German poem. Reynke consequently lies somewhat less than Reinaert did, but prevarication does not need to be stressed in his case, since he is no longer principally a politician. The exchange here is even further improved by being shortened. Reynke saves his account of what befell the rabbit and the female crow for a direct presentation to the court in Book Three.

He still tells Marten about his excommunication, and the ape proves to be just as corrupt as Reinaert portrayed him in the *Historie*. He will summon to Rome the provost who banned Reynke and arrange an annulment, meanwhile taking upon himself his nephew's guilt for having helped Ysegrym out of the monastery. Because Marten and Reynke are speaking privately, the fox will have to inform Nobel about this development when he addresses the court in Book Three, and Marten's wife Rukenauwe must support him voluntarily, since she does not hear her husband say that Reynke can count on her. Marten relates, however, that Nobel is already aware of the influence which he can bring to bear on the pope in order to effect an interdict, even though the mistress of the favored cardinal is not his niece anymore but only an acquaintance. As compensation Marten claims friendship with others who have His Holiness's ear. In conclusion the ape reminds Reynke that the king depends on their family (rather than merely on the fox) for advice.

The encounter with Marten terminates Book Two, as the second trial is about to start.

Book Three. A prose introduction states that the third
book shows three ways a ruler can fail to uphold justice: (1) by
not punishing a criminal; (2) by regarding a criminal's family;
and (3) by heeding lies. The implication of point 2 is that political
pressure is as strong in *Reynke* as in the *Historie,* and gloss III,4.7
also asserts that princes are often afraid to punish members of
powerful families. We will establish, however, that the fox's clan
does not significantly influence Nobel in the Low-German poem.
The Lübeck editor seems to have kept Hinrec's introduction to
Book Three despite changing the book's content in such a way
that its introduction is no longer quite suitable. Gloss III,4.7
must likewise have been taken over from the Missing Link.

Verses 4313–4432: Reinaert's first long declamation of his
second trial in the *Historie* (nearly ending Part One of the continuation to *Van den Vos Reynaerde*) had to be rewritten in *Reynke*
because of the actual conference with his uncle. The speech's
exordium is rather much the same as in the original, with the
fox asserting that his services have earned him the right to be
heard and that he would not have exposed himself to the danger
of execution if he were guilty. Reynke begins the body of his
oration by relating that Marten has restored him to the bosom
of the Church, and then he presents his version of what happened
to the rabbit and the crow, thus reversing the order in Reinaert's
speech. Without mentioning Pentecost (so that the contradiction
which resulted in the *Historie* is avoided),[20] Reynke essentially
retells Reinaert's story about the rabbit, but he claims that the
female crow choked to death on a fish bone instead of eating too
many maggots (probably because the latter allegation is more
dubious). Maybe her husband even slew her, he darkly speculates.
He skips the sections in the original prompting relatives to assist
him and threatening Nobel with an interdict, but he concludes
by challenging one and all to prove him guilty.

Verses 4511–22: Reinaert's incredible stupefaction at being
accused of Cuwaert's death in the *Historie* has been replaced in
the Low-German poem by a short speech based on lines 5261–69
and 5279 of the *Historie*. Without any hesitation Reynke responds
to Nobel's charge that he beheaded the hare by wailing, "How

can that be? Are Lampe and Bellyn both dead? Alas that I was
ever born!" He has lost the greatest treasure on earth, he cries,
and in contrast to Reinaert, who leaves open the question of
Cuwaert's killer, he blames the hare's murder on the late chaplain.
Bellyn, he says, must also have stolen the fabulous presents which
Lampe and the ram were supposed to deliver. Another flaw in
the *Historie* has been corrected, though at the price of some
repetition, as will be subsequently shown, and Nobel ought to
wonder whether Bellyn would really have brought the hare's head
if he had been responsible for severing it.

Verses 4523–4802: The king is at any rate so disgusted with
Reynke that he stalks out of the assembly hall while the fox is
still exclaiming over Lampe's death. He goes to his personal
quarters in the palace, where he finds Rukenauwe accompanying
the queen. Marten's wife immediately intercedes for her nephew,
although not at first in the most effective way, for she reminds
the king of how he used to esteem Reynke's father. Nobel could
reply that a parent's service fails to excuse a son's misdeeds, even
if the senior fox did not conspire against him. Rukenauwe dismisses the complaints which have been hurled at Reynke as the
slander of envious enemies.

To instill a more positive attitude in the king, she tells the
story about the man and the dragon, which Nobel admits he has
half forgotten (thus helping to warrant its inclusion in the Low-
German poem). Like her counterpart in the *Historie,* Rukenauwe
concludes her tale by contrasting the wise fox with the conceited
and selfish wolf and bear, though she only paraphrases the original
text. She does not go on at once to speak of Reynke's clan; the
point of her entreaty is that the fox should be pardoned rather
than just granted permission to speak; the queen and the leopard
(who is not even present) do not support her; and Nobel answers
her with a speech different from the conciliatory one spoken by
the *Historie*'s king. Instead of responding that a good alibi will
release Reynke, he says he will consider the case before rendering
a verdict but that he still views the fox as thoroughly bad. "I
don't know why you plead for that scoundrel," he growls to
Rukenauwe, whereupon she condenses verses 5078–5210 of the

Historie into a line and a half. The protracted introduction of
Reinaert's kin in the *Historie* is reduced to two short sentences.
"Listen to me, Sire," Rukenauwe warns. "Remember that
Reynke's family is great." Nobel then returns to his court, where
he surveys the fox's allies but gazes also at Reynke's enemies. He
is still his own boss.

The scene in the royal apartment is the most radical departure
from the *Historie* in the whole Low-German poem, because it
nearly eliminates political pressure on the king—that force which
is decisive in the *Historie*—although we must remember that
influential Marten has become Reynke's definite supporter. Instead of publicly confronting Nobel with what amounts to an
irresistible ultimatum, Rukenauwe, in a private tête-à-tête, leaves
him a great deal more freedom of choice. In doing so, she also
devolves upon her nephew the burden of securing release. By
impressing the lion with Reynke's value as an adviser, she makes
Nobel somewhat less hostile toward the fox, and she reminds the
king of political danger, but she does not virtually win Reynke's
battle for him, in contrast to what Rukenau accomplishes in the
Historie.

Verses 4803–31: The Low-German editor, or possibly Hinrec,
had a problem here—how to resume Reynke's trial. At the corresponding point in the *Historie* (where Nobel has nearly pardoned
Reinaert under Rukenau's coercion) the fox leads up to his description of the three gifts with a speech already used as the basis
for lines 4511–22 of *Reynke.* The editor decided to repeat those
verses, essentially, along with the king's accusation which elicited
them, because in the Low-German poem Nobel still intends to
execute Reynke for the murder of the hare, as he says in line
4814. Nothing could be more natural for the lion, upon returning
to the court, than to demand another explanation from the fox
of how Lampe was killed. (The editor may have meant to prepare
for the repetition by commenting in lines 4525–27, as Nobel
heads for his own chambers, "He was so angry that he didn't
listen carefully to what Reynke said.") The fox can likewise do
no better than to lament once more the loss of the would-be
presents. Again he also blames Lampe's death and the theft of

the valuables on Bellyn. Since Nobel does not indignantly exit this time and Rukenauwe has meanwhile joined the court, *Reynke* can resume its imitation of the *Historie*. Marten's wife asks her nephew to describe the lost heirlooms, and he does so, though not with Reinaert's prolixity.

Verses 5060–66: The passage in the *Historie* referring to Cleomades and the mechanical steed is practically deleted. Reynke merely states that the wood framing the mirror was like ebony, from which a horse was made "in Crompart's day" that could go a hundred miles an hour. The fox excuses himself from saying any more about the invention on the grounds that a full account would take too long. It is appropriate that Cleomades is no longer mentioned, since Reynke bears no resemblance to him. As we learned in regard to verses 4511–22, the Low-German fox does not share Reinaert's temporary inability to deal with Nobel; yet, for that reason, any allusion at all to the marvelous mount is now irrelevant.

Verses 5283–5392: The section on the healing of Nobel's father contains several slight changes. For example, Reynke Senior did not volunteer his services but was summoned after other physicians in the kingdom had been stymied, so that the elder fox becomes a more distinguished, but a less eager, benefactor. The really noteworthy innovations, however, are Reynke's claim that curing the lion is supposed to have been portrayed in the frame of the mirror and the omission of any explanation for why his father allegedly turned against Nobel after having waited upon the previous king so honorably (lines 5966–73 of the *Historie*). Either Hinrec or the Lübeck editor[21] must have felt that Reynke should not ask for trouble by unnecessarily reviving the now embarrassing conspiracy fabrication.

The heading to Chapter 12 maintains that the story of how the lion was cured is just another of the fox's lies. In the *Historie* the tale cannot be fictitious because the wolf is identified as Isegrijn and Isegrijn tacitly accepts it. In *Reynke,* on the other hand, the wolf is not named, so that the anecdote could indeed be untrue.

Verses 5393–5405: Before Reynke reminds Nobel of how much more generously he shared prey with the lion than Ysegrym did, a new, thirteen-line speech is given to Nobel, showing that a gradual change is taking place in the king. While Reynke's father may have been well deserved of the crown, says Nobel, subjects are always complaining about Reynke himself. Perhaps they are unfair, the lion adds, but he never hears anything good about the fox. Though not yet well disposed toward Reynke, His Majesty has nonetheless calmed down considerably since his irate vow in line 4814 to execute the nuisance.

Verses 5521–40: Nobel's speech absolving Reinaert from the murder of the hare (lines 6182–89 of the *Historie*) has been rewritten. The result is still the same, but the king's motives are somewhat different, in part because political pressure has been so greatly reduced in the Low-German poem. Presenting himself as a champion of natural law, Nobel says first that he will not treat anyone in a way which does not accord with what is right. Then he declares that he has forgiven Reynke on account of the latter's loyalty. In lines 5560–62, which are based on lines 6212–13 of the *Historie,* the editor adds a third reason, stating in effect that the king has once more succumbed to the fox's bribery. In gloss III, 14.2 we read that judges are often corrupted by the expectation of rewards but that Nobel is right in releasing the fox, given the lack of evidence at Reynke's second trial. Whether granting the fox the benefit of the doubt is insincere and merely camouflages greed is not clear. Being greedy in any case, however, Nobel should demand Reynke's entire treasure. His failure to do so is a shortcoming left over from the *Historie*.

Book Four.   Rather than open at the outset of Ysegrym's final denunciation of Reynke, the fourth book commences in the course of that tirade, oddly enough. It starts at the point where the wolf reports the rape of Ghyremod in the bog. The prose introduction implies that the rape is supposed to be stressed, and for two reasons. The first, which must be Hinrec's idea, relates to what is called the triumph of "wisdom" (actually cunning) over cupidity in the final book. Sly courtiers are reputed to cuckold their grasping foes. The second reason, which seems more characteristic of the Lübeck editor than of Hinrec, is that any type of adultery should be avoided, for it causes suffering. As evidence, both the Old Testament figure David and four verses ascribed to Augustine are cited, along with Ghyremod's and Reynke's troubles.

Verses 5855–78: As the fox begins his account of the visit with the she-ape and her brood in their squalid cave, he emphasizes that the subterranean demons are really not kin to him at all, even though he behaved as if they were. The Low-German editor had less cause than Hinrec to insert these lines, since Hinrec evidently meant his fox to be something of a model courtier in Book Four. He wanted to insure that his readers did not consider the future dignitary compromised by déclassé relatives. Perhaps for that reason he located the cave in Saxony (lines 5845 and 5861), figuratively expressing its residents' alien status by distancing them geographically.

Verses 6617–64: Reynke uses the fable about the scalded dog chiefly to discredit Ysegrym further instead of fair-weather friends. This change from the way the parable was applied in *Reinaerts Historie* makes it more consistent with the whole fourth book of the 1498 poem, which focuses on the conflict between fox and wolf. Just the beginning of Reynke's explanation of the apologue shows his shift in emphasis, for he says, "Sire, I'm talking about greedy fellows" (line 6644), whereas in the *Historie* Reinaert declares, "Sire, that's how flatterers are" (lines 7500–7501).[22]

Verses 6686–87: Besides naming Reynke chancellor of the empire, Nobel announces that he will refuse to hear any more complaints about the fox. There will be no further trials of Reynke. The immunity from prosecution implied by Reinaert's promotion in the *Historie* has been made explicit in the Low-German poem, probably in accordance with the Missing Link.

Verses 6811–22: In relating to his wife what occurred at court the second time, Reynke summarizes his definitive defeat of Ysegrym, which is not only political in the Lübeck epic but also juridical and sexual, insofar as the loser can bring no more charges against him and has been rendered impotent in their duel. Thanks to Hinrec, we may suspect, the fox says of Ysegrym, "I castrated him, so that he's of no use to the world anymore."[23] All of Ghyremod's cubs in the future will have to be her paramour's "stepchildren." The feud between fox and wolf, rather more developed in *Reynke* than in the *Historie* because of the early rape and the late report on the fight (plus even the different way in which the fable of the scalded dog is employed), becomes a greater unifying element in *Reynke* than it was in either the *Historie* or *Van den Vos Reynaerde,* running the length of the Low-German work like a spine.

Verses 6829–44: The Lübeck editor ends his epic with a statement of his purpose, which is to teach wisdom by exposing immorality. Both here and in glosses IV, 10.3–4, where we are admonished to learn wisdom, shunning greed and other faults, virtue is viewed as wise. By implication vice is considered foolish, reminding us of *Ysengrimus,* though Sebastian Brant's *Narrenschiff*—a review of sins and foibles hung with asses' ears—is bound to have influenced *Reynke*'s editor more. This *Ship of Fools,* translated into Low German, was printed by the "Poppy Press" at Lübeck in 1497.

Whereas *Reinaerts Historie* was chiefly concerned with politics, wisdom is what *Reynke* is about, but two conflicting levels of it have to be distinguished. The fox is Hinrec's "wise" adviser and the worldly-wise intrigant of gloss IV, 10.2 (described above, page 138), while the editor advocates a wisdom conducing to success beyond this life rather than within it.[24] The point of *Reynke,* in other words, is that its title figure's wisdom will be spurned by readers who are really wise.

By being 950 lines shorter than the *Historie,* more unified, more dramatic, and less flawed, *Reynke* was guaranteed broader appeal, even without its woodcuts and commentaries. Indeed, it had far and away the most success of any Reynard epic, being often reprinted, refashioned, and translated through the centuries. Even Goethe was attracted to it, dressing it heroi-comically in hexameters. Ascribing that popularity to the *Historie* rather than to *Reynke* has been a common mistake of critics and historians, most of whom have failed to perceive how much the latter work differs from the former. *Reinaerts Historie* did not enter world literature via Goethe's *Reineke Fuchs,* as Heeroma says, for example.[25] It was *Reynke de Vos* which did so. The Dutch fox moved to Lübeck to win his greatest victory—the triumph over time.

Chapter Six
Conclusion

Through 350 years in several countries and languages we have traced the main evolution of the medieval beast epic. Besides the principal or stem series consisting of *Ysengrimus, Branches* II-Va and I, *Proto-Reinaert, Van den Vos Reynaerde, Reinaerts Historie,* and *Reynke de Vos,* we have studied some particularly influential offshoots—*Branches* III, IV, V, VI, XIV, and XV—at least taken note of others, like *Reynardus Vulpes* and *Reynart the Foxe,* and hunted for roots. That a succession of literary works would develop one out of another over such an expanse of time is an interesting phenomenon in itself, but it is especially so when sections of the resulting tree are as individualistic as the seven poems which have most concerned us.

Utilizing earlier material, each of the six chief authors after Nivardus created something different. If we have read correctly, Pierre de Saint-Cloud shifted his criticism from greed per se to chivalry abused. Whereas Arnout defended the feudal order as a whole, Willem and the author of *Branche* I again attacked it, but with regard to themselves rather than in Pierre's impersonal manner. Even more than *Branche* I's author, Willem vented his resentment over the way in which society had dealt with him. The Lübeck reviser of *Reinaerts Historie* broadened its focus by construing the fox as a worldling rather than specifically as a politician. Not all Reynard epics convey a serious message, as we know from the *Roman de Renart,* but many minor specimens, whatever their concern, enrich a corpus of medieval literature already made intriguing by its major representatives.

Notes and References

Chapter One

1. See Ernst Voigt, *Ysengrimus* (Halle, 1884), pp. xxv, cxviii–cxx, and J. Van Mierlo, *Het Vroegste Dierenepos in de Letterkunde der Nederlanden* (Antwerpen, 1943), pp. 9–59, 113–18. E. P. A. Van Geertsom has argued in "Bruno de Auteur van de Ysengrimus," *Koninklijke Vlaamse Academie voor Taal- en Letterkunde* (1962):5–73, that *Ysengrimus*'s author was a certain Simon of Ghent and that the whole epic is what Donald N. Yates has called "a sort of *roman à clef*" (*The Cock-and-Fox Episodes of Isengrimus,* Dissertation University of North Carolina 1979, p. 47).

2. See for example Lucien Foulet, *Le Roman de Renard* (Paris, 1914), pp. 75–89.

3. See Voigt, *Ysengrimus,* p. 72.

4. See Léonard Willems, *Étude sur L'Ysengrinus* (Gand: Van Goethem, 1895), pp. 153–56.

5. Ute Schwab proposes a numerical explanation for the length of Book I on p. 242 of "Gastmetaphorik und Hornarithmetik im Ysengrimus," *Studi Medievali, serie terza* 10, pt. 2 (1969):215–50. More important was Nivardus's desire that Books I and IV be structurally similar. Each contains one-and-a-half episodes. At 1064 and 1044 lines, respectively, they also have nearly the same length. The fact that Books III and VII resemble each other in consisting of only a single episode apiece, moreover, suggests that Nivardus thought of his seven books as falling into two groups—the first three and the second four. In *De Civitate Dei* (11:31) Augustine declares that seven symbolizes totality or completeness, being the sum of three, the first wholly odd number, and four, the first wholly even one.

6. Franz Joseph Mone, *Reinhart Fuchs, aus dem neunten und zwölften Jahrhundert* (Stuttgart and Tübingen: Cotta, 1832).

7. Jacob Grimm, *Reinhart Fuchs* (Berlin: Reimer, 1834), pp. lxxi–lxxvii.

8. See Voigt, *Ysengrimus,* p. lix.

9. Ibid., p. lxxix. Cf. Ernst Voigt, *Egberts von Lüttich Fecunda Ratis* (Halle: Niemeyer, 1889), p. 182.

10. See Voigt, *Ysengrimus,* pp. 75–78, and Van Mierlo, *Dierenepos,* pp. 13, 90–93. L. Peeters is surely mistaken in linking Celebrant to Hildebrand, "Zu 'Ysengrimus', Liber Secundus VV. 69–70: 'Celebrand'," *Leuvense Bijdragen* 60 (1971):105–14.

11. See Kaarle Krohn, *Bär (Wolf) und Fuchs, eine nordische Tiermärchenkette* (Helsingfors: Finnische Litteratur-Gesellschaft, 1888), pp. 25–45.

12. Voigt, *Ysengrimus,* p. lxxx.

13. From August Hausrath, *Corpus Fabularum Aesopicarum* (Lipsiae: Teubner, 1959), 1, pt. 2:88–89.

14. See Karl Neff, *Die Gedichte des Paulus Diaconus* (München: Beck, 1908), pp. 191–96.

15. Winfried Trillitzsch, *Ecbasis Cuiusdam Captivi per Tropologiam* (Leipzig: Teubner, 1964), pp. 64–101.

16. See for example Karl Warnke, *Die Fabeln der Marie de France* (Halle: Niemeyer, 1898), pp. xliv–xlv. Fable 68 is on pp. 219–23.

17. Van Mierlo, *Dierenepos,* p. 60. Hans Robert Jauss, *Untersuchungen zur mittelalterlichen Tierdichtung* (Tübingen, 1959), pp. 100–101, exaggerates the passage's importance, taking it too seriously. I do endorse his statement, p. 101, however, that Nivardus's concept of fate is not meant to be anti-Christian.

18. This interpretation was first proposed by Van Geertsom, "Bruno," p. 10.

19. For an exception outside the genre of the beast epic see Grimm, *Reinhart Fuchs,* pp. xlvii–liii, especially p. li.

20. Regarding Nivardus's *caprea,* I side with Grimm against Voigt (*Ysengrimus,* p. 194), who calls for *Rehgeiss* ("roe") rather than *Gemse.* A roe would belong in Rearidus's clan, and the *caprea* of *Physiologus,* which *amat montes altos,* is rendered *Steingeiss* in medieval German. See Friedrich Maurer, *Der altdeutsche Physiologus* (Tübingen: Niemeyer, 1967), pp. 40, 41, 83. Mone's objection to *Gemse* on account of *die geographischen Grenzen der Thiersage* (Voigt, *Ysengrimus,* p. 194) is invalidated by Rufanus. Where a lion is king, a chamois can be baroness.

21. Bertiliana may be involved because of the proverbial hostility of *capreae* toward wolves, well-known from Horace's *Carmina,* 1:33, 7–8: *sed prius Apulis / iungentur capreae lupis.*

22. Voigt, *Ysengrimus,* p. xcvi.

23. The same inconsistency is repeated in the pilgrimage episode, ibid., pp. 235–36, lines 701–18 of Book IV. See also ibid., p. 247, lines 869–70 of Book IV. In the later revision of the sick-lion and pilgrimage episodes known as *Ysengrimus Abbreviatus,* the mistake is

eliminated. See Lieven Van Acker, "L'Ysengrimus Abbreviatus," *Latomus* 25 (1966):947, where the wolf does not pretend to be someone else.

24. Antti Aarne, *Die Tiere auf der Wanderschaft* (Hamina: Suomalaisen Tiedeakatemian Kustantama, 1913), pp. 152–56.

25. Van Mierlo, *Dierenepos,* p. 29, theorizes that Reinardus invented a mid-summer festival for a saint unknown to Sprotinus. Van Mierlo overlooked evidence, however, that Machutus has been honored on 11 July as well as on 15 November. See for example *Martyrologium Romanum* (Bruxellis, 1940), p. 525, section 7.

26. Hausrath, *Corpus Fabularum Aesopicarum,* 1, pt. 2:87–88.

27. Georg Thiele, *Der lateinische Äsop des Romulus* (Heidelberg: Winter, 1910), pp. lxii–lxiii, 110.

28. Grimm, *Reinhart Fuchs,* p. 420.

29. Leon Herrmann, "Gallus et Vulpes," *Scriptorium* 1 (1946–47):260–66.

30. Warnke, *Fabeln der Marie de France,* pp. 198–200.

31. Ibid., pp. 201–203.

32. Willems, *Étude,* pp. 108–11, 113; Van Mierlo, *Dierenepos,* pp. 32–34, 46–48.

33. See Voigt, *Ysengrimus,* pp. lxxxi–lxxxii.

34. Ibid., pp. xv–xvi, 305–306.

35. Krohn, *Bär (Wolf) und Fuchs,* pp. 89–92.

36. Warnke, *Fabeln der Marie de France,* pp. 224–26.

37. For another comic occurrence of the idea that consecrated bells will calm the elements, see my *Macropedius* (New York: Twayne, 1972), p. 102. Thomas Naogeorgus scoffs at the belief on pp. 124–25 of his *Regnum Papisticum,* 1553.

38. The best explanation of this reference to Ysengrimus's nose is Albert Schönfelder's, in *Isengrimus* (Münster: Böhlau, 1955), p. 155, note 4 to "Fabel IX." Regarding horse-head fiddles, see *Handwörterbuch des deutschen Aberglaubens* (Berlin: De Gruyter, 1934–35), 6:1667. Horse heads were placed on roofs to ward off evil spirits.

39. For related material see Voigt, *Ysengrimus,* pp. lxxxii–lxxxiii. In Nivardus's source the stork may have been a rooster and the setting, a stable.

40. Thiele, *Romulus,* pp. 162–66.

41. Hausrath, *Corpus Fabularum Aesopicarum,* 1, pt. 2:19–21, 78, 137.

42. Voigt, *Ysengrimus,* p. cxvii. Cf. Van Mierlo, *Direnepos,* pp. 84–86.

43. Jonas Balys, *Motif-Index of Lithuanian Narrative Folk-Lore* (Kaunas: Lithuanian Folk-Lore Archives, 1936), p. 9, no. 122, *E.

44. Hausrath, *Corpus Fabularum Aesopicarum*, 1, pt. 1:180–82.

45. See Thiele, *Romulus*, pp. 24–27.

46. Attempts to make sense of lines 421–22 of Book VII are misguided. After all, Salaura is making fun.

47. Schwab, "Gastmetaphorik," pp. 246–47.

48. Regarding both Walafried and Isidore, see Ernestus Duemmler, *Poetae Latini Aevi Carolini* (Berolini: Weidmann, 1884), 2:368–69.

49. Max Wehrli, "Vom Sinn des mittelalterlichen Tierepos," *German Life and Letters* 10 (1956–57):225, and Fritz Peter Knapp, "Materialistischer Utilitarismus in der Maske der Satire: Magister Nivards 'Ysengrimus,' " *Mittellateinisches Jahrbuch* 10 (1975):80–99. On p. 96 Knapp acknowledges Salaura's homily as a stumbling block for himself. What he and Wehrli read as expressions of irreligiousness are not to be taken at face value.

50. I agree with Teja Erb, "Pauper et Dives im 'Ysengrimus,' " *Philologus* 115 (1971):95, when she declares, "Die Hauptsünde ist für Nivardus die Sünde der Habgier. . . ." Although she does not cite Van Mierlo, he makes the same observation on p. 75 of *Dierenepos*. See also William Foerste, "Von Reinaerts Historie zum Reinke de Vos," *Münstersche Beiträge zur niederdeutschen Philologie,* ed. Felix Wortmann (Köln-Graz, 1960), p. 120.

51. H. W. Janson, *Apes and Ape Lore in the Middle Ages and the Renaissance* (London: The Warburg Institute, 1952), p. 184, remarks, "As a class, all large, long-necked fowl . . . such as the pelican, the *onocrotalus,* the crane, and the stork, seem to have been considered generically perverse or sinful during the Middle Ages. . . ." On p. 185 Janson adds that these birds "were also associated with the vice of gluttony."

52. Jauss, *Untersuchungen,* pp. 99–100.

53. See Max Manitius, *Geschichte der lateinischen Literatur des Mittelalters* (München: Beck, 1923), 2:582–87. The poem is in J. P. Migne, *Patrologiae Cursus Completus, Series Latina* (Parisiis: Migne, 1893), 171:1343–66.

54. Warnke, *Fabeln der Marie de France,* pp. 299–303.

55. Hausrath, *Corpus Fabularum Aesopicarum,* 1, pt. 1:125–26.

56. Van Geertsom, "Bruno," pp. 67–68.

Chapter Two

1. On both date and authorship see Foulet, *Roman de Renard,* pp. 217–37.

2. Ibid., pp. 100–19. See also John Flinn, *Le Roman de Renart dans la Littérature Française et dans les Littératures Étrangères au Moyen Age* (Toronto, 1963), pp. 16–18.

3. Ernst Martin, *Le Roman de Renart,* 3 vols. (Strasbourg, 1882–87).

4. See Foulet, *Roman de Renard,* pp. 239, 244–45, 251–52. It is doubtful that either XV or V was written for insertion into II-Va, since neither harmonizes with Pierre's epic and each is self-contained. Foulet's claim on p. 244 that Ysengrin would have no motive for attacking Renart in *Branche* V if V were not designed to succeed the rape scene in II-Va is invalidated not only by the author's possible presupposition of acquaintance with earlier *branches* but also by the fact that the wolf needs no motive, being *mauvais* (like Ysengrimus), as the fox states in line 8 of V.

5. See Martin, *Roman de Renart,* l:xxv.

6. Foulet, *Roman de Renard,* pp. 124–26, 143–56.

7. See Martin, *Roman de Renart,* 1:101, line 349; 104, line 472; 125, lines 1221–23; and 178, lines 641–42.

8. Warnke, *Fabeln der Marie de France,* pp. 154–55, fable 46.

9. Foulet, *Roman de Renard,* p. 153.

10. Warnke, *Fabeln der Marie de France,* pp. 47–49.

11. See Foulet, *Roman de Renard,* pp. 158–62.

12. Ibid., pp. 212–13. Pierre's audience did not need 1,000 lines to become acquainted with Renart.

13. See also Warnke, *Fabeln der Marie de France,* p. 40, fable 11, and Foulet, *Roman de Renard,* pp. 371–72, note 4.

14. See, however, Gunnar Tilander, "Notes sur le Texte du Roman de Renart," *Zeitschrift für romanische Philologie* 44 (1924):667, regarding line 1249.

15. See Foulet, *Roman de Renard,* pp. 218–26.

16. In Va, line 1075, Grimbert is said to be Renart's first cousin; in line 1154, his nephew. In *Branche* I they are consistently cousins. Although we will see much of Grimbert in subsequent epics, no badger figures in *Ysengrimus.* He is Pierre's invention.

17. See Martin, *Roman de Renart,* 1:187, line 954, and 3:174.

18. Pierre's contemporary Andreas Capellanus blames much warfare on love. See E. Trojel, ed., *Andreae Capellani Regii Francorum De Amore Libri Tres* (München: Fink, 1972), p. 330.

19. Juan Nogués, *Estudios sobre el Roman de Renard* (Salamanca, 1956), pp. 74–75, suggests that Pietro is derided as an exponent of Roman law.

20. Ysengrimus's cave and Ysengrin's in *Branche* II-Va also have a door that opens and closes.

21. Voigt, *Ysengrimus,* p. 301, line 742 of Book V. Reinardus is jesting, but he would not speak of his children if he had none. I disagree with Voigt, ibid., p. lxxix.

22. See Ernst Martin, *Observations sur le Roman de Renart* (Strasbourg: Trübner, 1887), p. 36.

23. Foulet, *Roman de Renard,* pp. 281–86.

24. See for example Krohn, *Bär (Wolf) und Fuchs,* pp. 46–54.

25. See Foulet, *Roman de Renard,* pp. 304–12.

26. MS H includes a different version of *Branche* IV after line 150, and in this variant the third chicken is remembered. See P. Chabaille, *Le Roman du Renart, Supplément* (Paris: Silvestre, 1835), pp. 113–21.

27. Lines 156 and 204 repeat line 439 of *Branche* II, where Renart wants Chantecler as badly as he wants water in IV.

28. It is surely meant to be incongruous that Renart also includes hawks and falcons (line 276), as if Ysengrin would have a bird catch his game in chivalric manner.

29. The author of the MS-H variant had more respect for Christianity. See Chabaille, *Supplément,* pp. 116–20. Note the change to *paradis terrestre,* which also occurs elsewhere—Martin, *Roman de Renart,* 1:214, line 616; 293, line 513, and 3:139, line 268.

In *Branche* XVII, when Noble's court believes that the fox has died and it is conducting his funeral service, Ferrant the horse describes his putative afterlife. His soul will enter heaven backwards, says Ferrant, and will be seated next to the she-ass on a bed composed of chickens, which he dare not harm. In that way he will atone for having been the bane of poultry on earth, the horse concludes (Martin, ibid., 2:224, lines 997–1012). Renart will therefore fare like a second Tantalus, the reward envisioned for him containing a bit of punishment. Ferrant's fantasy derives from the fox's in *Branche* IV. Paradise, which includes its opposite in XVII, becomes its opposite in IV, while in both works it is said to feature its prospective occupant's favorite food. Other examples of backward entrances in the *Roman de Renart (Branche* I, line 964; *Branche* VI, line 38; *Branche* XVII, line 1579) indicate that the fox's soul will be afraid on its arrival in Ferrant's version of the beyond, and it has good reason to be. Its juxtaposition with the *arnesse* is probably meant to suggest Renart's duplicity (even though the she-ass is not described as *fauve*). See *Branche* I, line 1291; *Branche* VI, lines 161–62; and Arthur Langfors, *Le Roman de Fauvel par Gervais du Bus* (Paris: Firmin-Didot, 1914–19), p. lxxxiv.

30. *Handwörterbuch des deutschen Aberglaubens* (Berlin: De Gruyter, 1927), 1:1677–80.

31. The scene may have been prompted by Nivardus's monastery episode, especially since the prior wields a candlestick (line 409).

32. This is the first time in the *Roman de Renart* (provided *Branche* V antedates XIV) that an animal really wears clothes of any kind.

33. The fact that the cricket lacks a name in *Branche* V (except for line 180 of MSS C, M, and H) indicates that V is older than I.

34. Foulet, *Roman de Renard*, pp. 250–51.

35. Ibid., pp. 249–50.

36. Ibid., pp. 314–15.

37. Ibid., p. 316.

38. Hausrath, *Corpus Fabularum Aesopicarum*, 1, pt. 1:36–37, and Horace's Epistles, 1:7, lines 29–33.

39. The similarity to *Branche* V could be coincidental but probably is not, justifying the assumption that V antedates XIV. See Foulet, *Roman de Renard*, p. 320.

40. Pierre mentions a *Dant Galopin . . . li levres* in line 1083 of *Branche* Va, Martin, *Roman de Renart*, 1:190.

41. For example, can Brun go all the way back to court *fuiant . . . plus que le trot* (line 702), having lost the hide from his front feet, if he is not indeed *esporonant* (line 705)?

42. Foulet, *Roman de Renard*, p. 256, is mistaken in saying that Tibert and Renart are mounted in the first half of XV. A *esperon* in line 182 is not meant literally.

43. Canterbury pilgrims were claiming in the 1170s that Thomas à Becket's tomb was thaumaturgic, and Louis VII visited it in 1179 (the year *Branche* I was probably written) to secure the recovery of his ill son Philip Augustus.

44. For example, Robert Bossuat, *Le Roman de Renart* (Paris: Hatier, 1967), pp. 113–14. The passage in question is Martin, *Roman de Renart*, 1:15–16, lines 505–30.

45. See Foulet, *Roman de Renard*, p. 333.

46. See Naoyuki Fukumoto, *Le Roman de Renart, Branches I et Ia* (Tokyo: Librairie France Tosho, 1974), pp. 202–203, regarding line 740 of that edition.

47. Jacob Grimm and Andreas Schmeller, *Lateinische Gedichte des X. und XI. Jh.* (Göttingen: Dieterich, 1838), pp. 340–42.

48. See Foulet, *Roman de Renard,* pp. 336–38. Cf. Voigt, *Egberts Fecunda Ratis,* pp. 195–96.

49. See for example Gaston Paris, *Mélanges de Littérature Française du Moyen Age* (Paris: Champion, 1912), pp. 413–14. Jauss (*Untersuchungen,* p. 264, note 1) maintains that Renart heeds Noble because he is a *Schelm,* yet even rogues avoid being hanged.

50. In lines 417–29 of *Ecbasis Captivi* the fox feeds the panther who has brought word of developments at court, and after leaving home he prays for pity, a safe return, and the wolf's defeat.

51. One is reminded here of the fox claiming senescence in lines 473–80 of *Ecbasis Captivi,* as mentioned in Chapter One, regarding the sick-lion episode of *Ysengrimus.*

52. Fere is not in evidence at court until the fox is about to leave (line 1440). At his arrival, for instance, he greets only the king.

53. The author did not know that Nur-ud-din had died in 1173.

54. Tardif's debut in the *Roman de Renart* occurs at Copee's funeral, in which he participates because *Branche* I's author needed *limacons* to rhyme with *lecons* (lines 409–10). Having created Tardif, the author could not resist the comic contrast which results from radically altering a snail's proverbial pace. That intentionally absurd anthropomorphism probably inspired the even better example of tongue-in-cheek topsy-turviness found in *Branche* XVII, where Couart rides a horse with a captured peasant around his neck (Martin, *Roman de Renart,* 2:198–200, lines 61–108). Not only has the normally craven captor reversed his nature like the speedy snail; he has also switched roles with his catch. The peasant is a furrier, who customarily treats hares as the hare is treating him.

55. Whether the chase in *Branche* I is on horseback is ambiguous. Cf. *Branche* XVII's imitation, Martin, ibid., pp. 226–30. In both I and XVII Tardif carries a banner. Note the resemblance of Renart at the end of I to Walwein in lines 11741–78 of Wace's *Brut.*

56. Lines 9, 23, 480, 610–11, 833, 892, and 1499. Negative auctorial comments about Renart had become a tradition, begun by Pierre de Saint-Cloud, who was sincerely critical of the fox.

Chapter Three

1. *Branche* X and *Rainardo e Lesengrino,* each of which was surely written by only one author, are also influenced by *Branche* I as far as the trial and then depart from it for a completely different ending, but

even up to the trial they are much more independent of I than is *Van den Vos Reynaerde.*

2. We will not deal, however, with the question of stylistic differences in *Van den Vos Reynaerde,* studies of which have proved inconclusive. See J. W. Muller, *Van den Vos Reynaerde* (Leiden: Brill, 1939), p. 80, note 22. Throughout, the verse form is couplets with four beats per line.

3. The edition used is W. Gs. Hellinga's *Van den Vos Reynaerde* (Zwolle, 1952).

4. Cf. lines 30–32 of *Moriaen,* 13–14 of *Karel ende Elegast,* and 1–4 of *Ferguut.*

5. In contrast to MSS F and B, A gives "Malcroys" rather than some form of "Manpertuus" as the name of Reinaert's home in line 273, but all MSS agree that he has more than one burrow. "Malcroys" derives from "Malcrues." See note 14 to Chapter Two. Like Renart in *Branche* I, Reinaert does actually live in a den, which is often referred to as a castle (or as a house).

6. F. Lulofs, *Nu Gaet Reynaerde al Huten Spele* (Amsterdam: Thespa, 1975), p. 75, argues that Coppe cannot be interred until the morning of the second day. Perhaps Arnout does not allow enough time for ceremony and preparation, but he nevertheless indicates, lines 421–64, that no break occurs.

7. The author of *Reinaerts Historie* (MS B) has the fox talk less fearfully with Bruun outside his burrow, where he can communicate better.

8. Since Renart does not comment on Brun's paws in *Branche* I, Arnout may have been thinking of *Ysengrimus,* lines 1131–32 of Book III, Marie de France's fable 68, or *Aegrum Fama Fuit.*

9. The pejorative phrase in line 544 expresses Reinaert's opinion, not Arnout's. In line 640 Arnout calls Bruun a *keytijf* without the adjective *arm.* His reference to Bruun in line 778 and all of lines 872–73 can also be read as sympathetic. The author of *Branche* I commiserates with Brun only to the extent of referring to him as *li las* in line 608.

10. Gerard-H. Arendt, *Die satirische Struktur des mittelniederländischen Tierepos "Van den Vos Reynaerde,"* Dissertation Köln 1965, p. 234.

11. Martin, *Roman de Renart,* 1:50.

12. Ibid., 2:29–39. Cf. ibid., 1:268–69, lines 126–34.

13. Ibid., 3:28, line 1051.

14. Compare line 1820 with line 537 of *Branche* I, ibid., 1:16, and 3:14.

15. It does so even in the different version of the trial contained in MSS B and H. Ibid., 3:35–37.

16. Lulofs, *Nu Gaet Reynaerde,* p. 49, suggests that by having *de hoogste adel* dispense retribution Nobel is attempting to appease the fox's clan.

17. Martin, *Roman de Renart,* 1:57–58.

18. Cf. *Branche* VI, lines 1363–64, ibid., p. 235.

19. Cf. *Branche* VIII, lines 113–19, ibid., p. 268.

20. In line 2714 he speaks as if he were really related to the wolf.

21. In *Reinaerts Historie* the badger supposedly told his wife (not mentioned in *Van den Vos Reynaerde*), and she told Hermeline—a process which is psychologically sounder.

22. See Thiele, *Romulus,* pp. 84–88. Reinaert's stork was originally a snake.

23. In *Âventiure* 19 of the *Nibelungenlied* Hagen purloins Kriemhild's treasure to forestall an attack on Gunther.

24. Cf. *Branche* I, lines 1088–92, Martin, *Roman de Renart,* 1:31.

25. In line 1433 of *Branche* I Renart breaks a straw as a sign of reconciliation with Noble. Martin, ibid., p. 40.

26. The description of this godforsaken locality may have been suggested by Isaiah 34:10–11, concerning the cursed land of Edom. See Arendt, *Satirische Struktur,* pp. 115–17. Arendt makes too much of the similarity, however.

27. Rijn and Cuwaert's counterfeiters, led by a dog whose name differs in every MS, have proved quite puzzling. Lines 2667–83 probably constitute private jokes about a couple of Willem's personal acquaintances rather than cryptic comments on anything in *Van den Vos Reynaerde.*

28. Martin, *Roman de Renart,* 1:384–87, lines 1529–1614.

29. Ibid., p. 226, lines 1066–67.

30. The idea may have been that one earned salvation by helping to sustain the Latin Kingdom of Jerusalem. In *Reinaerts Historie, over zee varen* is not a part of Master Gelis's teaching, and a penitent must act *bi des priesters rade.*

31. See lines 60, 614, 956, 1077, 1175, 1700–1701.

32. Lines 2218, 2842, 2981, 3277.

33. See Hubertus Menke, *Die Tiernamen in Van den Vos Reinaerde* (Heidelberg: Winter, 1970), pp. 122–23.

34. According to line 3382 the queen is still present at court, but she no longer speaks.

35. According to R. B. C. Huygens, *Reynardus Vulpes* (Zwolle, 1968), p. 166.

36. Arendt, *Satirische Struktur,* p. 293.

37. Whereas MS B agrees with F that Willem "made *Madoc,*" MS A states that he "made many books."

38. In place of MS F's "Arnout," A repeats the name Willem (line 6), which makes no sense. Cf. *Branche* I's prologue.

39. Huygens, *Reynardus Vulpes,* p. 25. A. Welkenhuysen argues for 1279 in "A Latin Link in the Flemish Chain: The *Reynardus Vulpes,* its Authorship and Date," in *Aspects of the Medieval Animal Epic,* ed. E. Rombauts and A. Welkenhuysen (The Hague: Nijhoff, 1975), pp. 125–26.

40. The latest of the *Roman-de-Renart branches* likely to have influenced either Arnout or Willem are XII, dating from the 1190s, and Ia, written circa 1190–95. (See note 2 to Chapter Two.) Arendt, *Satirische Struktur,* pp. 20, 61–64, justifiably rejects the ever persistent arguments for a composition date as late as the 1260s on account of similarities between *Van den Vos Reynaerde* and other works. Allowance must be made for coincidence, standard stylistic formulas, copyists, and the likelihood of at least as much influence *from* Arnout and Willem as *on* them, within medieval Dutch literature. Hans Wiswe, "Meybom to Aken," *Jahrbuch des Vereins für niederdeutsche Sprachforschung* 87 (1964):72, says in connection with *Reynke de Vos* that after 1220 anyone excommunicated longer than six months was to be outlawed by secular authorities—a policy of which Nobel is ignorant.

Chapter Four

1. See Ernst Martin, *Reinaert* (Paderborn, 1874), pp. xx–xxi. Martin's edition is the one we will use.

2. On the elimination of much courtly diction see Foerste, "Von Reinaerts Historie," p. 118.

3. K. Heeroma, *De andere Reinaert* (Den Haag: Bert Bakker, 1970), p. 130, has proposed emending *quaet* in line 1404 to *raet,* and the prose *Historie* supports him (Hellinga, *Van den Vos Reynaerde,* p. 85). Even so, Grimbaert is still in cahoots with his uncle, and line 1304 of *Reynke de Vos* keeps *quad.*

4. Grimbaert's duplicity is anticipated in *Branche* XVII of the *Roman de Renart,* where Grimbert assists the fox in avoiding a summons by pretending to have died. When reporting the bogus death to Noble, the badger even weeps. See Martin, *Roman de Renart,* 2:240–42.

5. Ibid., 1:197–240.
6. Regarding Grimbert, see ibid., p. 210, line 467. Admittedly, when describing Brun's entrapment (lines 231–96), Noble does not say that the bear was a royal messenger.
7. Cf. Ecclesiasticus 10:9 and line 432 of *Branche* III, Martin, *Roman de Renart,* 1:143.
8. Cf. lines 2007–15 of *Branche* Ia, ibid., p. 56.
9. According to M. W. J. A. Jonckbloet, *Étude sur le Roman de Renart* (Groningen: Wolters, 1863), pp. 373–75, Bernart represents a real religious of the same name, favored by France's King Philip Augustus, so that contemporary listeners to *Branche* VI could readily believe that he would have enough influence on the lion to save Renart.
10. Certainly the *Historie*'s author did not mean for Grimbaert and Reinaert's other nonvulpine kin to be hunted by Isegrijn and Bruun, despite Firapeel's words in lines 3452–56.
11. Martin, *Roman de Renart,* 2:67, lines 861–89, and 235–38, lines 1400–1519. Both crows in XVII complain of Renart at court, perhaps causing the inconsistency with Scerpenebbe.
12. All Latin in the sequel seems to have been written properly, even though in his revision of *Van den Vos Reynaerde* the *Historie*'s author left Arnout's broken Latin phrases uncorrected. Willem did not include any Latin, except for one word, *dominus,* in line 2065, nor is there any in the denouement to *Van den Vos Reynaerde.*
13. Gaston Reynaud and Henri Lemaître, *Le Roman de Renart le Contrefait* (Genève: Slatkine, 1975), 2:241–43. The moral occurs elsewhere, as in *Cento Novelle Antiche,* or *Il Novellino,* no. 94.
14. Flinn, *Roman de Renart au Moyen Age,* p. 521.
15. In lines 4286 and 4287 Grimbaert even quotes from lines 51 and 48, respectively, of his counterpart's equivalent speech in *Branche* VI.
16. Nobel borrows a proverb from the lion in *Branche* VI, as noted by Martin, *Reinaert,* p. xlii. Cf. Martin, *Roman de Renart,* 1:199, lines 88–90.
17. See Maartje Draak, "Is Ondank's Werelds Loon?" *Neophilologus* 30 (1945):133.
18. Adenet le Roi's *Cleomades.* The episode in question is from lines 2377–2706.
19. See Garmt Stuiveling, *Esopet* (Amsterdam: Hertzberger, 1965), 2:25–26, fable 20. Cf. ibid., 1:20, note 5.
20. Ibid., 2:21, fable 17, and 1:20, note 5.
21. Warnke, *Fabeln der Marie de France,* pp. 315–18, fable 98.

22. See Stuiveling, *Esopet,* 2:11, fable 8, and 1:20, note 5.

23. Regarding sources of "The Squire's Tale," see Charles Larson, "*The Squire's Tale:* Chaucer's Evolution from the Dream Vision," *Revue des Langues Vivantes* 43 (1977):602.

24. In lines 69–70 of *Ysengrimus Abbreviatus* (Van Acker, "L'Ysengrimus Abbreviatus," p. 927), the wolf recommends that the sick lion eat the liver of Berfridus the goat and Joseph the wether. See also ibid., p. 920, note 2. In his *Natural History,* Book 28, sections 193, 197, 230, and 247, Pliny prescribes wolf liver as a cure for various ailments. Léopold Hervieux, *Les Fabulistes Latins* (New York: Franklin, 1960), 2:304–305, reprints a fable in which the sick lion thinks a seven-year-old wolf is needed as medicine and "Ysengrinus" protests that he is not even three.

25. Reinaert appears to have forgotten that his father is supposed to have committed suicide. See lines 5971–72.

26. Martin, *Roman de Renart,* 2:188–90.

27. Stuiveling, *Esopet,* 2:60–61, fable 52.

28. For sources of this stratagem see Martin, *Reinaert,* p. 405, note to line 6815, and Flinn, *Roman de Renart au Moyen Age,* p. 313.

29. *Branches* XIII and XVII of the *Roman de Renart* also contain duels in which the fox loses, being in the wrong. Martin, *Roman de Renart,* 2:99–106, 232–34.

30. For a similar, historical incident from twelfth-century Flanders, see H. C. Lea, *Superstition and Force* (New York: Blom, 1971), pp. 178–79.

31. In contrast to C and P, MS B contains a verse (7586) which proves that Nobel has not been deceived at all and is merely playing politics. See Hellinga, *Van den Vos Reynaerde,* p. 334.

32. Heeroma, "De Tweede Reinaert," pp. 115–51 in *De andere Reinaert.*

Chapter Five

1. They prepared the *editio princeps* not only of *Reynardus Vulpes* but also of Nigel's *Speculum Stultorum.* See John H. Mozley and Robert R. Raymo, *Nigel de Longchamps Speculum Stultorum* (Berkeley and Los Angeles: University of California Press, 1960), p. 15.

2. Huygens, *Reynardus Vulpes,* pp. 10–11.

3. N. F. Blake has edited Caxton's translation under the title *The History of Reynard the Fox* (London, 1970).

4. See Willy Steinberg, *Reinke de Vos* (Halle, 1960), pp. 259–65; Hellinga, *Van den Vos Reynaerde,* pp. 91–119. Krogmann, "Die Vorlage des 'Reynke de Vos,' " *Jahrbuch des Vereins für niederdeutsche Sprachforschung* 87 (1964):35–38, argues that a slightly different version of Leeu's verse *Historie* was published between 1480 and 1486, but the case is weak and improbable, resting on *laster* in line 1737 of *Reynke* versus *tachter* in line 175 of the Cambridge Fragments. The Lübeck editor simply read *tachter* as a misprint for *lachter,* despite Krogmann's protest on p. 36 against such an easy, natural explanation. See Niclas Witton, "Die Vorlage des Reinke de Vos," *Reynaert Reynard Reynke,* ed. Jan Goossens and Timothy Sodmann (Köln-Wien, 1980), pp. 129–30.

5. See Martin, *Reinaert,* p. xxii, and Krogmann, "Die Vorlage," pp. 38–42. Witton, "Die Vorlage," *Reynaert Reynard Reynke,* p. 107, maintains that the Missing Link is not the immediate source for *Reynke,* but his supporting arguments are dubious. Judging by the Cambridge Fragments, for example, he assumes on pp. 56 and 58 that Hinrec was not inclined to invent anything. See my review of *Reynaert Reynard Reynke,* dealing with Witton's essay in detail, in the *German Quarterly* 55, no. 2 (1982):245–47.

6. Thirty of its woodcuts were probably copied from the Missing Link, in fact. See Timothy Sodmann, *Reynke de Vos* (Hamburg: Kötz, 1976), pp. vi–xi.

7. See Olaf Schwencke, "Ein Kreis spätmittelalterlicher Erbauungsschriftsteller in Lübeck," *Jahrbuch des Vereins für niederdeutsche Sprachforschung* 88 (1965):20–58, and Timothy Sodmann, *Dat narren schyp* (Bremen: Schünemann, 1980), p. 23.

8. The edition of *Reynke* used here is Steinberg's. See note 4 to this chapter. For linguistic evidence that *Reynke*'s first prologue comes from the Missing Link see Heeroma, *De andere Reinaert,* p. 204.

9. See J. W. Muller, "Mr. Henric van Alcmaer," *Tijdschrift voor nederlandsche Taal- en Letterkunde* 7 (1887):251–60, and D. Th. Enklaar, "Hendrik van Alkmaar," *Tijdschrift voor nederlandsche Taal- en Letterkunde* 50 (1931):315–22.

10. Squirrels (*ekerken*) are numbered among both servants and merchants.

11. Ernst Martin, *Das niederländische Volksbuch Reynaert de Vos* (Paderborn, 1876), p. 5–6.

12. Heeroma, *De andere Reinaert,* pp. 198–99. The heading to *Reynke*'s *ander vorrede* (Steinberg's edition, p. 4) was probably taken over from the Missing Link, and Heeroma is probably wrong in asserting that Hinrec did not split his preface in two. See *De andere Reinaert,* pp.

200–201. The main purpose of Hinrec's second prologue—nearly lost in *Reynke*'s equivalent—must indeed have been to explain the four-book structure.

13. See Lambertus Okken. *"Reinke de Vos* und die Herren Lübecks," *Niederdeutsches Wort* 11 (1971):7–24. C. Scheffler, "Die deutsche spätmittelalterliche *Reineke-Fuchs*-Dictung und ihre Bearbeitungen bis in die Neuzeit," in *Aspects of the Medieval Animal Epic,* p. 90, and Hubertus Menke, "Ars Vitae Aulicae oder Descriptio Mundi Perversi?" *Jahrbuch des Vereins für niederdeutsche Sprachforschung* 98–99 (1975–76):122–25, reason that the first edition of *Reynke* has to have been expensive.

14. Foerste, "Von Reinaerts Historie," p. 110, lists twenty-eight passages in *Reynke* and the chapbook that supposedly agree, but some are doubtful. On pp. 113–14 he attempts to show that a number of Hinrec's commentaries were based on remarks in Balduinus's *Reynardus Vulpes.* The evidence is inconclusive, though Hinrec may well have known *Reynardus.*

15. For many minor changes in *Reynke* see Foerste, ibid., pp. 128–43. He is not always correct, however.

16. See Steinberg, *Reinke de Vos,* p. 236.

17. He may be different from the cat's assailant in *Reynke,* and he wields simply a long staff instead of a crosier (line 711). In general the Lübeck editor toned down satire on members of the clergy. See Foerste, "Von Reinaerts Historie," pp. 137–38.

18. Ibid., p. 145, and Raimund Vedder, "Die Illustrationen in den frühen Drucken des Reynke de vos," in *Reynaert Reynard Reynke,* pp. 205, 214.

19. The remark was also deleted from the prose *Historie.* See Hellinga, *Van den Vos Reynaerde,* p. 226, and Blake, *Reynard,* p. 52.

20. Cf. Martin, *Das niederländische Volksbuch Reynaert de Vos,* p. 77, indicating that Hinrec had already dropped Pentecost. In the prose *Historie* the contradiction was avoided differently. See Hellinga, *Van den Vos Reynaerde,* p. 7 (*omtrent pinxteren*) and Blake, *Reynard,* p. 6.

21. Hinrec is the better candidate, having been more political. Another consideration is the fact that the 1564 chapbook also dispenses with an explanation for Reinaert Senior's treachery. See Martin, *Das niederländische Volksbuch Reynaert de Vos,* p. 96. That omission could be coincidental, however, since in the same episode the chapbook and *Reynke* disagree regarding other details.

22. In extant MSS of the *Historie, losenghier* (Martin's emendation) is written *lose ghier* (*lose ghieren* in the prose *Historie*), indicating that

reinterpretation of the fable was begun by copyists, before Hinrec and the Lübeck editor. See Hellinga, *Van den Vos Reynaerde,* p. 331.

23. In *Branche* Ib of the *Roman de Renart* Ysengrin is castrated by a mastiff, and in a report to Hermeline which concludes the poem her mate takes credit for that excision. See Martin, *Roman de Renart,* 1:72, 89–90 (lines 3197–3208, especially 3205–3206).

24. Whereas in line 6790 the fox praises wisdom over gold, the editor, alluding to that line in gloss IV, 10.3, states that *de lerer* also praises wisdom over gold. The same expression is therefore used in both antithetical ways.

25. Heeroma, *De andere Reinaert,* p. 116. Heeroma echoes Muller, *Van den Vos Reinaerde,* p. 53.

Selected Bibliography

PRIMARY SOURCES

Blake, N. F. *The History of Reynard the Fox.* Early English Text Society, 263. London: Oxford, 1970.

Hellinga, W. Gs. *Van den Vos Reynaerde.* Zwolle: Tjeenk Willink, 1952.

Huygens, R. B. C. *Reynardus Vulpes.* Zwolse Drukken en Herdrukken, 66. Zwolle: Tjeenk Willink, 1968.

Martin, Ernst. *Das niederländische Volksbuch Reynaert de Vos.* Paderborn: Schöningh, 1876.

————. *Reinaert.* Paderborn: Schöningh, 1874.

————. *Le Roman de Renart.* 3 vols. Strasbourg: Trübner, 1882–87.

Steinberg, Willy. *Reinke de Vos.* Altdeutsche Textbibliothek, 8. Halle: Niemeyer, 1960.

Voigt, Ernst. *Ysengrimus.* Halle: Buchhandlung des Waisenhauses, 1884.

SECONDARY SOURCES

Flinn, John. *Le Roman de Renart dans la Littérature Française et dans les Littératures Étrangères au Moyen Age.* Toronto: University of Toronto Press, 1963. A survey of medieval literature influenced by the *Roman de Renart.*

Foerste, William. "Von Reinaerts Historie zum Reinke de Vos." In *Münstersche Beiträge zur niederdeutschen Philologie.* Niederdeutsche Studien, 6. Edited by Felix Wortmann. Köln-Graz: Böhlau, 1960, pp. 105–46. The most important attempt to distinguish *Reynke de Vos* from its predecessors.

Foulet, Lucien. *Le Roman de Renard.* Paris: Champion, 1914. The cornerstone of recent *Roman-de-Renart* research.

Jauss, Hans Robert. *Untersuchungen zur mittelalterlichen Tierdichtung.* Beihefte zur Zeitschrift für romanische Philologie, 100. Tübingen: Niemeyer, 1959. An influential examination of medieval animal literature as a whole.

Knapp, Fritz Peter. *Das lateinische Tierepos.* Erträge der Forschung, 121. Darmstadt: Wissenschaftliche Buchgesellschaft, 1979. Chapter 2 provides a good overview of *Ysengrimus* research through 1976.

Muller, J. W. *Van den Vos Reinaerde, Exegetische Commentaar.* Leiden: Brill, 1942. The best commentary on *Van den Vos Reynaerde.*

Van Mierlo, J. *Het Vroegste Dierenepos in de Letterkunde der Nederlanden: Isengrimus van Magister Nivardus.* Antwerpen: N. V. Standaard-Boekhandel, 1943. The soundest lengthy study of *Ysengrimus.*

Witton, Niclas. "Die Vorlage des Reinke de Vos." In *Reynaert Reynard Reynke.* Niederdeutsche Studien, 27. Edited by Jan Goossens and Timothy Sodmann. Köln-Wien: Böhlau, 1980, pp. 1–159. The latest study of *Reynke*'s lineage.

Index

DATE DUE
